Ridge

By Tarin Breuner

Dedicated to my horse Whisper, who has always been my escape from life's stresses.

Prologue

"And she swings her arm back and then at just the right angle she releases and . . ." I pulled my arm in and tossed the horseshoe, "Yes! It circles *flawlessly* around the post," I turned back and smiled at Cade, "For the third time in a row, might I add."

"Now don't be getting cocky, you're good but I'm better," Cade walked a few feet back and threw two more horseshoes around the post. "And I'm the one who taught you, might *I* add," he winked at me, landing his last throw just as expertly.

"And if you were a better teacher, I'd be able to outplay you." I put my hand on my hip.

"You can't outplay someone who never misses a shot," Cade said, mimicking my hip position and flipping his imaginary ponytail mockingly.

"Alright, then we'll up the challenge." I pointed to an adjacent open-wall structure, the spot where the ranch often held barn dances. "We'll climb on the roof and throw from there," I smirked, "You in?"

"Always," he said picking up the horseshoes and handing me half. "Race you to the top!" Cade said, shoving me to the side and kicking up dust as his boots bounded through the thick dirt. I sprinted after him and jumped on his back as soon as I caught up.

"Cheater!" I yelled. He spun in a tight circle until I went flying off and landed, laughing, on my butt.

"That'll leave you nice and sore in the morning," Cade winced, offering his hand to pull me up. I took it between both my hands and used all my might to try and pull him down despite the fact he was a year older and a foot taller. He pretended to stumble for a minute before yanking me to my feet easily with the strength of a ranch worker. I kicked a cloud of dirt in his direction.

"Hey!" Cade said.

"You deserved that," I asserted. He laughed, holding up his arms in defense. I sat down on the wooden bench to the side of the structure and pulled my jeans back over the tops of my hickory-colored boots. Cade sat next to me and laid his head back to look up at the sky. The stars speckled across the darkness as far as the eye could see. It always made me feel calm, to look at the sky, how little we are in comparison. We sat there for a few minutes in relaxed silence.

"Rev!" My mom's call broke the quiet.

"I guess it's time for me to head in," I said beginning to walk back towards my cabin. I quickly turned back around and pointed at Cade. "But don't think you're getting out of that rematch, it's still gonna happen."

"I'll be ready," Cade smiled, hands resting in the front pockets of his dirt-clad wranglers.

*   *   *

My hazel eyes fluttered open at the sound of rattling outside my window. Then a gentle, tap, tap, double tap, three more taps. I pushed the covers off and opened my blinds.

"Hey Cade," I said as I turned to stretch.

"Hey," he said leaning on my window pane, his amber eyes sparkling against the pre-dawn sky while his caramel skin and dark locks blended into the shadows. "We've got to hurry if you want to make the sunrise, so get dressed quick." I ran into the other room to pull jeans and a flannel on over my tank top. Walking back in I secured my medium-length, ash-blonde hair into a simple braid and grabbed the boots from beside my bed.

"Let's go," I said, beginning to throw my legs out the window. Cade caught my arm on the way down and we began racing towards the barn.

"Start tacking up Grayling," Cade said while handing me my horse's lead rope. "I'm going to go get Gallatin from the pasture."

"Hey there Gray," I said rubbing along her beautiful dun coat. She trailed behind me as I led her away and tied her to the post outside the tack room with a daisy loop knot. Walking inside, I breathed in the sweet fumes of molasses and worn bridles. I threw a hackamore around my shoulder, slipped a few horse cookies in my pocket, and carried a western saddle between my arms.

As I smoothed the seat down on Grayling's back I smiled at my name etched on the side of the saddle-skirt: "rev" in little beige stitching. Cade had surprised me with it a couple summers back, after my family had started making this trip a yearly tradition.

I put my left foot in the stirrup, wrapped my hand around the saddle horn and swung my leg over. As I sat on Grayling's back waiting for Cade, I reached over her shoulders and began braiding down her silvery mane. The cool morning breeze tugged at my flannel, pulling it back against my shoulders.

Within minutes, Cade trotted over on his beautiful black stallion, Gallatin. He was a broad-chested mustang with a bright blaze down his forehead.

"Ready?" Cade asked.

"Yep," I said, squeezing my thighs for Grayling to walk forward. I followed Cade out of the barn area and we continued on the mother-path towards the woods.

"Where are we going this time?" I asked.

"It's your last morning here, where do you think we're going?" Cade smirked.

"I guess I just want to forget that I'm going back home today," I said, looking down at the horn.

"You'll be back soon, you always are," Cade said. "And then in a few years, you'll be working here." I smiled at the thought. It had been my dream since I first came to the ranch, at seven years old, to work here after I graduated, and now, going into my freshman year of high school, it was only a few years away.

"Now, let's see if you remember how to find your way," Cade halted Gallatin and looked back at me: "You lead." I held up my head confidently and trotted ahead of him on the trail. We continued on and I made a left at the first fork.

A little while later, we made it to our destination: the ridge, our favorite spot on the ranch, where you can see everything. Cade and I dismounted and tied our horses to nearby trees so that we were free to sit in the grass near the edge. The sun had made it halfway up the mountains and the sky was a gorgeous confusion of rose, lavender and gold.

"It sure is called Big Sky Country for a reason, huh?" Cade remarked. I gazed out at the endless horizon.

"It's breathtaking," I sighed. "Nothing will ever compare."

*   *   *

We were silent on the ride back down, not wanting to admit that summer was over. When we got back to the barn, Cade swung off Gallatin's back and led him away, leaving me to say my good-byes to Grayling.

I kissed her nose as tears threatened the backs of my eyes. She put her forehead to my chest and began rubbing, breathing hot air out her nostrils. I smiled softly and hugged her neck. A few minutes later, I turned at the sound of shuffling behind me. Cade stood there waiting.

"You can leave her in here for now and I'll come back to put her away," he said. I nodded, patting her neck one more time before turning away to start walking back to the cabins.

When we got back my family was in a flurry grabbing suitcases and putting them on the porch. Cade immediately got to work helping with the bags as I ran to my room to gather my last few things. My mom caught my collar as I rushed by.

"I know you wanted to ride one more time but you were supposed to be back half an hour ago to help pack," she said, crossing her arms.

"I know, I'm sorry, I lost track of time," I bit my lip. "Again." My mom rolled her eyes and laughed.

"Go get the rest of your stuff. Tripp's going to be here with the car in a minute and we can't be late for our flight."

Back outside, the truck had already pulled up and everyone was piling the luggage into the bed. Tripp walked over and put his hand on Cade's shoulder. They could be twins if not for the four-year age difference. Two half-Latinos toned and tan from work on the farm, with their mother's smile and their father's eyes.

"Cade, dad wants your help back at the house before you meet the wranglers this morning," Tripp said; Cade nodded and walked over to my parents.

"Myrine, Van, always nice to see you," he said, giving them both hugs.

"Take care Cade," my dad said.

"Come here Clay." Cade smiled at my little brother. They did their special handshake and Cade ruffled his dirty blonde hair. Clay laughed and got into the truck, as did my parents, leaving me standing there alone. I shrugged when Cade looked at me. We both smiled and came into a tight embrace. I climbed up into the cab next to my brother and stuck my head out the window. Cade was waving us off.

"See you next summer!"

1

"You will have to finish reading *Our Town* over break as you will have a cumulative test the first day back and don't forget about your written response assignment either. It may be your last book of the year but that doesn't mean that you can start slacking off now," my English teacher, Mrs. Widman said, back turned to us, as she wrote on the board. My eyes drifted to the clock as I twirled my pen against its accompanying notepad, having finished both the book and the response, weeks ago. The hands of the clock ticked forward, closer and closer until the bell finally rang. I picked up everything from my desk and tossed it in my backpack; making a right turn at the door, I went straight for my locker. Just as I was switching out my last book, I saw my best friends, Brenn and Leslie, walking towards me.

"So Rev, what are you up to this break?" Brenn asked.

"Relaxing," I said, with slight exasperation. "Enjoying my last free week, since I have to leave for the honors program at Duke the day after we graduate," I said.

"When do you commit officially?" Brenn asked.

"A month from today." I offered a closed mouth smile.

"I forgot how early you have to leave," Brenn frowned. "And it's all the way across the country, ugh, I don't want you to go!"

"Neither of us do, but," Leslie cut in. "Even so, we're very happy for you."

"Yeah of course," Brenn jumped back in. "Gosh I remember back when all you talked about was working on some ranch and now here you are on your way to the same prep school that your parents went to." She looked off and smiled, her eyes bright. "You must be so excited!"

"Uh yeah," I hesitated. "Of course, I mean it's such an amazing opportunity, who wouldn't be excited, right?" I smiled a little too big and Leslie gave me a sideways glance, crossing her arms.

"Anyways, I should get going," I said, starting to back away before turning directly into a tall blonde with deep blue eyes.

"Mitt, hey!" I said, then realizing I was stepping on his foot. "Oh gosh, sorry," I said while moving off.

"No worries, it's not the first time, you never were the most graceful person," he laughed. I blushed, looking at the ground.

"Anyway," he said, touching my arm. "I hope you have a good break, you deserve it." He gave me a smile and looked over my shoulder. "See you guys around," he said, heading down the hallway. I turned to see who he'd been looking at. Leslie and Brenn stood there, staring wide-eyed with gritted teeth. When they saw me look over, they immediately busied themselves examining the books they had in hand. I sighed and crossed my arms.

"Guys come on, you don't have to be all weird about it. Obviously I'm gonna see him, we go to the same school. But seriously our break-up was mutual, no hard feelings. There's no reason to make a big deal about it."

"Okay." Brenn put up her arms. "But if you need an ice cream, girl's night during break," she smiled. "You know we're around for you to call us."

"Absolutely," Leslie added, putting her arm around my shoulders. "And just for the record sweetie, you didn't need us to make it awkward, you two did that perfectly well on your own."

"Well thank you," I laughed. "I appreciate the support. So now I'm gonna actually head out and hopefully not run into anyone else," I said, pointing my thumb to the side of my shoulder. "Have a good break!" I called, waving my hand as I walked away.

*   *   *

When I got back to my house I was surprised to see that our yard was empty. There was never a day after school when Clay didn't have a baseball team's worth of his sixth-grade friends playing a sport of some kind, on the front lawn. I pulled the key out from the top of my bag and unlocked the front door, letting it swing open as I walked inside.

"Hi Kody, hi baby." I kneeled to the height of our German Shepard – Golden Retriever mutt. He pawed my knees before running off to look for his ball. I got up from the ground and swung my bag back over my shoulder. "Hello?" I called, crossing the front room and heading into the kitchen. My mom and dad were leaning against the island talking, when I walked in.

"Hi honey!" My mom said catching my eye and laying her mug down on the counter. "How was your last day before break?"

"It was good, you know, just the usual." I shrugged sheepishly, picking an apple out from our fruit bowl. "You guys are home oddly early . . ." I said, taking a bite of the apple as she made no effort to respond. "And where's Clay?" I continued. As if on cue Clay came bounding into the room clutching a small black suitcase.

"Hey dad, I was almost done packing and then I remembered I don't have a suitcase . . . so can I borrow one of yours?" He asked motioning to the one in his hand.

"Sure thing kid," my dad laughed.

"Packing? Where are you going?" I asked. Clay turned back to my parents.

"You haven't told her yet?" he said.

"I was just about to, dear," my mom smiled.

"What's going on?" I said, tossing my apple core in the compost.

"Well," my mom started. "It's the spring break of your senior year and that's a big deal. You leave for school right after graduating and it could be the last break where we are all together, so your dad and I felt that we should be doing something special, going somewhere."

"Going somewhere? What, like camping?" I asked.

"No, a bit further than that," my dad said.

"We're going back to the ranch!" my mom said.

"Wait, what?" I said, genuinely caught off guard.

"We used to go all the time and it's been years now, we thought it would be great to go back one last time," my mom said. Clay was jumping around excitedly.

"I can't wait! I'm gonna go finish packing!" he said, running out of the room.

"Wow," I breathed.

"What's the matter, aren't you excited?" my dad asked, "You've always loved it there."

"Yeah! I mean of course I am, I do love it there," I agreed. "I'm just so surprised that's all."

"Well, you're going to have to get over your shock fast and start getting your stuff together," my dad said. "We leave for the airport at eight tomorrow morning."

"Um, yeah, okay, I'll go start packing!" I started walking away but turned back and gathered my parents in a hug. "Thank you," I said. "I know this is for me." My mom kissed my forehead,

"Of course, after how hard you've worked, you deserve a trip. We're so proud of you."

"We can't wait to see you in a Duke sweatshirt in just a matter of weeks!" my dad added.

"Me either." I gave a quick smile before pulling back and leaving the room.

I ran my hand along the banister as I slowly ascended the stairs. At the top, I opened the hall closet and pulled out a suitcase before walking two doors down and turning into my room. Quotes adorned my brick-tone walls and books of all shapes and sizes decorated shelves on each side. I slid my closet door open and began tossing clothes on my pink-grey comforter. Shirts, flannels, jeans, jackets . . . I counted in my head as I undid hangers.

Crossing the room to search for a book, I found myself eye-to-eye with my acceptance letter from Duke. I abruptly turned the frame face down, took a breath and busied myself by riffling through the stacks and picking out a novel to add to the pile.

Absentmindedly, I began folding and tucking until I had moved everything from my bed to the suitcase. As I pressed my palms on the top and started moving my hand towards the zipper, I thought about what I could be missing. Suddenly, I moved away, knelt to the ground and began rummaging through the stuff under my bed. When I reached the middle, I moved a coat to the side and drew out a medium-sized plastic bin. Blowing dust from the top, I removed the lid and placed it on the floor beside me. I took out a pair of dark brown boots with white lacing along the sides. I ran my hands along their worn soles and moved to the side to pull them on. I turned my ankles in circles and stretched out my toes; it felt good to have them on again. I shifted back to the bin and searched to the bottom. When I peered down, my heart stopped for a second. I reached in and brought out an old photo album. Leaning against the wall, I held it in my hands with delicate care. The front cover of the album was garnished with simple horseshoe stickers encircling the words "Kix Ranch" written in brown ink. I turned through it gently, taking a moment for each page. The barn, the horses, the game area, fireworks from the year I was there during Fourth of July.

When I was about halfway through, I couldn't get myself to move past a specific photo. I felt tears welling in my eyes as I stared at the picture. It was of me at the top of the ridge. I remembered the day Cade had taken it; I wasn't looking at the camera. Mid-sentence talking to him I was looking out across the fields, smiling so wide the corners of my mouth threatened to reach the bottoms of my eyes. A natural flushed pink in my cheeks as the wind tugged at the hairs in my braid. The happiness was so natural and genuine, like there was nowhere I'd rather be. I couldn't remember the last time I had looked like that.

2

The sound of a barking dog exploded in my ear, jolting me awake. I reached across the bed for my phone, silenced the alarm, and stuffed my head back into the pillow.

"Rev! Help!" I heard Clay screaming from the hallway.

"What's wrong! Are you okay?" I blindly stumbled out of bed and ran towards him, rubbing my eyes.

"Yeah I'm good, but we leave in a half hour and you needed to wake up," he said, smiling smugly. I blew the hair out of my face, shoved him to the side, walked back in my room and shut the door.

I walked to my closet, grabbed a brush off the dresser and combed through my caramel hair. After pulling on a pair of jeans and a cream-colored capped-sleeve shirt, I bent down to lace up my old blue Converse. They had swirly designs and words drawn all around their beat up rubber-sides. I smiled at the little mountain sketch I had done years ago.

When I looked up I saw my suitcase sitting across the room, zipped and ready to go. I sighed and bit my lip as I grabbed it by the top handle and carried it downstairs.

"Rev honey, what took you so long? We have to leave in a few minutes! Here, eat this," my mom said, handing me a cinnamon-apple muffin.

"Sorry mom I ---"

"Lost track of time?" she cut in.

"You know me so well," I smirked. Clay scrambled around the living room picking up games and DVDs and stuffing them in his carry on.

"Clay, what are you doing? You know the ranch doesn't have TV or internet."

"Yeah, but we have twenty minutes to the airport and after that the two plane rides it takes to get there. Something's gotta occupy me!" I rolled my eyes and took the last bite of my muffin.

"Okay kids, let's go, let's go!" My dad rushed in out of nowhere, and herded me and Clay towards the door. My mom followed behind, grabbing her purse from the table as we climbed into the car. My dad started the motor and we were on our way.

*　　*　　*

We burst away from security and rushed to find our gate on the terminal board, of course we would get the farthest one. Our parents grabbed us by our arms and we all started running through the terminal.

My bag kept slipping off my shoulder as I awkwardly ran with both it and a rolling carry on.

"Rev, here's ten dollars, go buy us some waters and then run over to meet us at the gate," my mom said, shoving a bill in my hand.

"What, mom! What if I miss it?"

"You're not gonna miss it, just hurry!" My family rushed on towards the end of the terminal, leaving me in the midst of a crowded hallway of travelers. I rolled my eyes and made a quick turn back towards the mini-general store. I swiped four bottles from the cooler and got in line, tapping my foot anxiously. Person after person seemed to take twice as long as necessary to check out as my eyes were watching the minutes tick by, on the clock across the store. When I finally got to the front, the cashier took his time punching in the numbers; he looked up and smiled.

"How are you doing today?"

"Fantastic," I said through gritted my teeth.

"That's good to hear, we've been pretty busy, a lot of travelers." I shrugged politely as he handed me back the waters.

"Thanks," I said gathering them in my arms. He looked down to pull out the receipt.

"So where are you headed to—" I heard him say over my shoulder, but I was already out the store and running back down the hall.

"Excuse me, excuse me, sorry, excuse me!" I said, repeatedly bumping into people along the way. I got to the gate within minutes of the doors closing. Last to get on the plane, I scanned the rows until I saw my mom had covered the seat next to her with a jacket. Plopping down on the seat, I handed out waters and tucked my bag underneath on the floor. No sooner had I fastened my seat belt when the flight attendant started talking from the front of the plane.

"We played it a little tight on time, but we're fine," my mom said, putting her hand on my knee. I raised an eyebrow and gave her a sideways glance.

"Really is just like old times, huh?" she laughed. I looked across the aisle at my dad and Clay playing a game of tic-tac-toe, then out the window as the plane started moving down the runway.

"Yeah," I said, "It really is."

3

"From the back roads to the Broadway shows with a million miles between

There's a least a million love songs that people love to sing

And everyone is different and everyone's the same

So this is just another way of sayin' the same thing . . ."

Randy Travis' voice rang out from the radio as our car wound through the mountains of the Gallatin Gateway. Clay sat next to me in the back seat, headphones on, looking down at the game on his phone. My parents were chatting away with Tripp at the front of the car, as I kept my eyes glued to the immense landscape.

Montana, the sprawling untouched beauty, the never-ending sky: it made me realize how much I had truly missed it, and even after all these years, I felt right at home. My heart got fuller the farther into the mountains we went. But that joy did not stop the growing sense of butterflies I got the closer we drove to the ranch.

As we made our turn onto the off-road, I looked out to see the old wooden horseshoe-clad sign: "Kix Ranch" it read, making me think back on all the years and trying to add up how many times I'd read that same sign.

The gravel flew out from under the tires as we pulled around the final turn, leading us towards the cabins. Tripp put the car in park and started pulling our bags from the trunk as we all climbed out and took in our surroundings. I closed my eyes and took a deep breath of the fresh mountain air. Clay immediately ran inside while my dad went back to help Tripp carry in the luggage. I stood with my mom, gazing at the cabin.

"It's funny. I guess after all this time, I just thought maybe something would have changed, but everything's the same," I said.

"You should never change something that you already love. Just think, if it were different, it might not hold the same place in your heart," my mom told me. I looked at her curiously, but before I could say anything more, a voice rang out from behind us.

"Hello, Bere family!" I turned to see a beautiful dark-haired woman with Spanish skin, smiling at us, clipboard in hand. An orange and white corgi sat obediently at her feet.

"Layton!" I cried. She laughed as I ran at her for a big hug. She smoothed my hair down and held my face in her hands. I bent down to pet the dog, "Hi there, Tilly," I said.

"My goodness Rev, it's been far too long," she said before bringing me back in for another hug. She looked up to see my mom and embraced her with open arms. "The woman herself. I cannot even begin to tell you how happy I was when you called to make a reservation, when you guys stopped coming it felt like we were missing part of the family."

"Well, I admit, it took us a while," my mom said. "But we couldn't be happier to be back, and just in time too. Rev will be graduating just over a month after we get home."

"I heard, and I must say, congratulations," she smiled at me. "Now if I could just get you to come back here after school's out and work for us, like we always used to talk about, well, everything would be perfect." Layton put her hands on my shoulders. My mom laughed.

"I'm afraid she's got a bit more schooling after this," she said, looking at me with a glint in her eye. "She will be attending Duke you know. My alma mater!"

"Is that so? Well my goodness, that's a change!" Layton said. "I'd love to hear all about it."

"Of course, we have so much to catch up on!" my mom said.

"We do. I have to get back to the office now but I will make sure to find you at dinner so we can chat." Layton looked down at her clipboard. "Hey, is my brother still in there?"

"Yes, he and Van are in there somewhere, do you need him?"

"If you could just send him my way whenever he's done, I have a few scheduling things to go over with him."

"No problem," my mom said. "I'll go see what they're up to now, it was great seeing you, Layton. I'll talk to you more tonight," my mom said, heading up the steps of the cabin. Layton was starting to turn away when she stopped and looked back at me.

"Hey Rev," she said. "I think Cade's still out working in the arena. I know how excited he is to see you, you should go by when you get the chance." And with that, she went back to the office and left me standing there. I stood there for a minute before running up the steps and peeking my head around the door frame. My mom walked out of the bedroom and sat down on the couch with a magazine.

"Hey mom," I said. "I'm gonna go over and say hi to the horses."

"Mmhm," she said without looking up, "I'm sure it's the horses that you are going to look for . . ." she raised an eyebrow. When I didn't say anything she looked up and said, "Well, what are you still doing here? Go!" I smiled and ran back out the door.

I made my way across the ranch and arrived at the barn. Dozens of horses were spread all throughout massive corrals as others were lined up inside, ready for a trail ride. But to the side of all of that, a gorgeous black mustang galloped through barrels in the arena. The rider was practically glued to the saddle, one with the horse. I slowly walked closer, watching the delicate movement of the horse's muscles and the gentle touch of the rider's legs against its sides. The horse stopped short as the rider leaned back and moved the reins back and forth to get the horse backing up, they then did small circles with only the front legs moving before the reins were released and the horse was offered pets as reward. I saw the rider lift their head in my direction and then suddenly the horse was at a gallop again, driving across the arena to where I stood. I walked even closer, as the rider pulled the horse to a stop and swung their legs off in one swift movement. The horse stood in place obediently as the rider came within feet of me. His amber eyes stared at me with an expression I couldn't read.

"Hi," I breathed.

"Hi," he said, swallowing. "You're taller."

"Yeah, five-six now," I responded.

"So I'm only like what, eight inches taller now?" He broke into a cheeky smile. His dark hair cut short and his Spanish skin even tanner than in the past.

"Whatever," I rolled my eyes.

"It's good to have you back," he said. "We've missed you around here."

4

When Cade went to put Gallatin away I slipped off and hurried back to the cabin. Closing the door quickly as I came inside, my mom looked up from where she remained on the couch.

"Back so soon?" she asked with a puzzled expression.

"Uh yeah, I just wanted to say a quick hi to the horses," I lied. "But now that I have, I'll just go ahead and unpack," I said, awkwardly pointing in the direction of my room.

"Okay," my mom said, tentatively. I made a beeline for my room and shut the door as soon as I got inside. I breathed deeply, and collapsed on my bed, ignoring the suitcase on the ground to my left.

After a while, through my window, I saw Cade walking across the grounds, looking around confused before turning in to the main lodge. I rolled on my back and shoved a pillow in my face, letting out a sigh.

There was a knock on my door, but without waiting for a response, my mom came in the room. I watched her eye my empty closet and the full bags still sitting next to it.

"You did a wonderful job unpacking," she said, crossing her arms with a tilted head. I gave a quick smile and gritted my teeth. "What's going on?" she asked.

"Nothing," I said, but I knew she didn't believe me. Some moments of silence passed when a large bell rang out across the ranch.

"Looks like it's time for dinner, so I guess if nothing's wrong, you're good to go right now?"

"Well nothing's wrong . . . but I am feeling really tired and kind of have a headache, so if it's okay, I would actually just rather skip dinner tonight." My mom looked at me skeptically,

"Rev, are you sure that's what it is? I mean honey, this trip is for you, after all!" she said, with slight irritation in her voice.

"I know, and I'm so excited to be here. I can't thank you enough, really, I just need some rest. But by tomorrow, I'll be good!" I said, hoping it was true.

"Okay," she said. "Get some rest, I'll check on you when we get back."

"Sounds good," I said, relieved. After they had gone, I did eventually unpack, but spent most of my time distracting myself by re-reading *Our Town*.

A while passed when I lifted my head at the sound of tapping. That familiar tap, tap, double tap, three more taps. I couldn't help but smile, but made sure to fix my expression immediately before pulling up the window.

"What are you doing here?" I asked. Cade was standing there in the grass looking up at me.

"Well you just kind of walked off earlier, and then you weren't at dinner. I was worried something might be wrong."

"I'm fine, just tired," I responded, not looking him in the eye.

"Can I come in?" he asked. Then, holding up something wrapped in tin foil, "I brought cornbread," he held up a tin tray and smiled a sideways grin. "I remember it's your favorite."

"Thank you," I said. "But I really think I should just rest a little. I'll see you tomorrow though." I moved to close the window again.

"Wait," Cade said. "If you want to rest fine. But at least take the cornbread," he held it up to me through the window.

"Okay," I said, taking it in my left hand. "Thank you," I said, leaving the window before he had a chance to respond.

*   *   *

Even after my family got back, I didn't leave my room much that night. They thought I was asleep but I stayed up for hours just watching the fan rotate in circles above my head. I had taken the photo of me at the ridge out of the album and laid it across my chest, letting it move up and down with each breath.

5

The next morning, I shuffled behind my family on the way to the lodge for breakfast. I would occasionally hold my forehead in an effort to keep up my act of illness whenever my mom looked in my direction.

Walking through the door, I almost ran directly into Cade as he was trying to exit. He smiled when I looked up at him.

"Hey, how you feeling?" he asked.

"Um, pretty good, still a little worn out but better than last night," I said. He looked over my shoulder then turned back to me with a smirk.

"Your family left, you don't have to lie anymore," he said, crossing his arms.

"Huh?" I turned to see that my parents and brother were already halfway through the buffet on the other side of the room. "Oh," I said. "Well I'm not lying. I never said I was sick, I just had a headache, that's all."

"Aha, sure," he said. "I don't know why you're doing it but even if they're buying it, I'm not," he said; I looked at the ground. "Anyways," he started, "Your first official day back on the ranch. What are your plans?"

"I don't know, just hanging out I guess," I said, shrugging.

"Well then," he said, "How about we get you back on a horse? Meet me at the stables in an hour?"

"I mean, I ---" I stammered.

"I'll take that as a yes," he said, backing out the door before I could give a real answer.

*   *   *

Sure enough, I swallowed my pride and made my way down to the barn after breakfast. Just as I was stepping on the railing to search the horses grazing in the pasture, Cade came around the corner, with Grayling trailing behind.

"Gray!" I cried, leaping off the railing and burrowing my face in her neck.

"So how come I didn't get that kind of reaction when you first saw *me*?" he smirked.

"Because you're not a horse," I said, kissing Grayling's muzzle. "How come you were already walking her out here? You didn't even know I was gonna come."

"Yeah I did," he handed me her lead rope. "I think we both know after all this time you weren't gonna pass up a chance to ride, and besides wouldn't you rather go out like this then wait for the group trail rides in a couple of hours?"

"Huh," I said. "Well then, you better go get Gallatin so we can get out of here."

I groomed Grayling thoroughly, enjoying the warmth of her coat in the sun and the long circles I made with the brushes' stiff bristles. She let me comb through the small tangles that were gathering in her mane, I could feel Cade watching me from the opposite side, where he stood with Gallatin.

Together we went into the tack room and threw bridles over our shoulders. I tucked a blanket under my arm and went to the back wall where the saddles displayed themselves in rows. Cade grabbed the rest of what he needed and headed for the door when I stopped along the wall at a familiar honey-colored saddle.

I smoothed my hand across the worn old stitching and stopped when I saw "rev" sewn on the back. The same saddle I'd ridden in, years before. "You still have this?" I turned to Cade in surprise.

"Yeah, of course I do," he shrugged sheepishly. "I still have everything."

I turned back to hide my blushing cheeks and slipped the saddle over my arm. I brushed past him back towards the horses, evading his eyes all the while.

We rode out to Cawdrey Creek, a few miles west of the barn. There wasn't much talking on the way there, just the sound of the breeze pulling through the pine trees. We went there slowly, allowing me plenty of time to take in the surroundings: the bright green grasses, the tall tightly-packed trees creating a canopy above, the thin winding dirt trail on which we traveled. I took in heavy breaths, sinking deeper in to my saddle with every exhale.

The babbling sound of the creek became clearer and clearer until we reached a small meadow glade along the water. Climbing off the horses, we led them to the side where we could tie them to nearby trees.

"Doesn't matter how much time I've spent here, it always amazes me how beautiful everything is," I said, looking about.

"Even living here, you never quite get over it," Cade responded, walking over to the creek and squatting down to run his hands through the water. I went and stood next to him, watching as a dragonfly flew right over the top of his arm. Suddenly, Cade made a quick move with his hand, looking up at me smirking, and splashed me with the creek water.

"Hey!" I said, then moving to shove him off balance and into the water. As he lost his footing, he kicked up water at me and grabbed my hand to pull me down with him. I screamed as I landed in the cold water but lifting myself out of it, it was really quite refreshing. Cade was drenched, his clothes and hair sticking tight to his skin. Skin cold, and cheeks flushed, we continued throwing fake-angry splashes at each other until our eyes met and we couldn't help but start laughing.

"What are we doing?" I said, climbing up on the bank of the creek and twisting the water out of my hair.

"Uh, having a water fight?" Cade said, sitting across from me.

"No," I laughed. "I mean, what are we doing? What are we doing acting like strangers?"

"I don't know," he said. "But hey, I've been trying to change that."

"I know, and I've done nothing. I'm sorry," I said, looking at him. "I was just nervous, and worried, I guess."

"Worried about what?"

"Worried to find out that we aren't the friends we used to be," I said, keeping my eyes on the grass blade I was twisting between my fingers.

"Come on Rev, that couldn't happen," he said. "When you have that kind of connection with someone it doesn't just go away."

"Yeah," I said, "You're right, it's stupid, I don't know, I just need to get it out of my head." I fell backwards on a bed of flowers and closed my eyes, letting the sun beat down through the trees and dry my skin.

"That's what nature's for," Cade said; I smiled.

"Yeah, I guess a place like this is good for that, huh?" I pulled my body up to a sitting position, rolling my neck side to side. When I looked over my left shoulder, I saw two dandelions next to each other in the patch of grass. I pulled them, one at a time, from the soil, holding one out for Cade and clutching the other protectively.

"Make a wish," I smiled. He laughed and we both blew until each seed had flown off with the breeze.

"Well?" Cade looked at me.

"Well what?" I asked.

"Well what'd you wish for?"

"I'm not telling you!" I said.

"What! Why? You just said you wanted to get back to the way we were and we used to always tell each other what we wished for," he said.

"Yeah, but that was when we were wishing for things like getting to stay out later and birthday presents," I explained. "Those were little things, this is bigger than that, and I really want this one to come true."

"The little things are always the big things," Cade said. I rolled my eyes,

"You know of all the things I missed, your random quotes of wisdom were not on that list." Cade started laughing and I shoved him to the side as I stood up to walk back towards Grayling.

*   *   *

Back at the barn, Cade and I untacked the horses and released them in the pasture to graze with the rest of the remuda. Walking back, I threw the halter over my shoulder and wiped the dirt off my face with the sleeve of my shirt.

"You and your family will be at the campfire tonight, right?" Cade asked.

"Yeah, we should be," I said. "I don't think Clay would ever pass up s'mores."

"I could have guessed that," Cade laughed. "Here, I'll take the halters back. I have some other chores to do down here anyway," he slipped the halter off my shoulder and hung it on his arm.

"You sure you don't need any help?"

"Yeah, I'm good, you go ahead. I'll see you tonight."

"Okay, thanks," I said, then turning into him to give a quick hug. A look of surprise flashed across his face, then he just smiled.

"Bye." I pulled away and headed back up the path towards the cabins.

6

That night, after dinner, Clay and I trotted along the gravel path leading to the campfire. Our parents trailed behind us, arm in arm. It had gotten dark and the stars were beginning to pop up all across the sky. The smell of melting chocolate and burning wood filled the air as we heard a gentle crackling sound grow louder and louder. We turned the corner to find the pit already half full with guests sitting on logs and a fire growing higher with every minute as it cast a gentle orange glow over the faces of onlookers.

My parents went and sat in the back with Layton and Dante, Cade's dad and the owner of the ranch. Clay and I found room on the end of a front log across the circle. I rubbed my shoulders, harvesting the warmth of the nearby fire.

Three border collies weaved their way through the logs, collecting pets at each one. When they reached us, I immediately recognized two, Crosby and Conway; they had been ranch dogs for as long as I could remember. They were brothers, each with a marbled-grey coat and navy blue bandana. Crosby picked up a stick off the ground and Conway happily took the other end; together they ran off to wrestle in the nearby grass. When I turned back around, I saw that the third dog remained; this one was brown and white with a red bandana. He sat on the ground next to me as I stroked his head.

Clay began making s'mores, holding out sticks two at a time. The kids sitting next to us were all friends he'd made on his group ride this morning. Before long, they were all chatting, and making up campfire stories. Clay started reminiscing and recounting memories from our previous trips out here.

"One time, we were out on a ride, and we saw a pack of wolves," Clay said with an animated expression. The kids watched him with wonder. "They had dark grey hair and bright yellow eyes and they —"

"Well Clay, that was cool, but that was nothing compared to that time there was a grizzly," Cade said, as he came up from behind us and sat on the ground by the fire.

"You saw a grizzly?" one girl asked. She wore he hair in two braids and had bright blue eyes wide with a mixture of fear and amazement.

"Sure did," Cade said, "Tell them Clay."

"It, it was really big and it was golden colored and it was by a creek when we saw it and then it –"

"And then it started chasing us," Cade said. Clay looked at him and he winked.

"Right, right, it started chasing us and we had to get the horses going really really fast, and we were going through woods –"

"Until," Cade cut in, "Clay had the idea to turn off into a meadow, thinking if we ran in zig zags, we could confuse the bear until it ran out of energy, 'cause Clay remembered that, although a bear is faster than a person, or even horse, it doesn't have nearly as much stamina," Cade said knowingly. "And his plan worked! The bear got tired and we got away just fine, right Clay?"

"Right yeah, good thing I had that idea huh?" he smirked. All the kids were yammering excitedly saying things like *wow that's amazing; you're so smart* and *tell us again how it went*. They all surrounded Clay and went off to the side a little bit, asking more about his bravery in a close-call bear encounter. With them all standing up, it left plenty of room for Cade to get off the ground and take a seat on the log. I looked at him with narrow eyes.

"Nice," I said.

"Nice, what?" he asked defensively.

"You just lied to a bunch of kids!" I said, spreading my arms.

"I merely exaggerated, making your brother look *way* cooler, by the way," he said. "We did see a grizzly together one time, you know, on the other side of the ridge," he smiled, taking a sip of his drink. I rolled my eyes and shook my head, then looked back down at the dog.

"Who's this new guy?" I asked, motioning to the brown border collie that remained nearby.

"That's Raid," Cade said. "We rescued him last year. He'd been abandoned, came here and fell into patterns right away. He's a good boy," Cade said proudly. We looked over and saw that Raid was pawing at the graham cracker box, when one popped out. He snatched it quickly and lay down with it caught between his paws.

"He does have a habit for stealing food, however," Cade said; I laughed.

Tripp walked to the front of the fire, guitar in hand and took a seat on the center log, a spot always left open, unless for him or Dante. He began tuning and strumming mindlessly for a few minutes without saying anything. Then he started that famous lead up to "Sweet Home Alabama" immediately following with "American Pie." The same way he starts every campfire. By the end, everyone was singing along. He looked up at smiled at the group.

"Well now that we've got our voices warmed up," he laughed. "Any requests?" He turned his head towards me, "Rev?"

"You already know what I'm gonna say," I called out.

He laughed and went right into strumming, "We've got some Tom Petty coming your way," he winked. "*She's a good girl, loves her mama . . .*" he started. I put my hand to my heart and sang along, obnoxiously loud. Cade smiled and laughed before joining in. The other voices were hesitant for the first few lines but by the chorus, everyone was all in: "*. . . And I'm free, free fallin'; Yeah I'm free, free fallin'!*"

7

Walking down the food line, I reached over my mom's hand to get a scoop of the fresh fruit mix. We continued on to the end, where I picked up two pieces of cornbread. Clay was off eating with some friends, and my dad was helping Dante with something, so it was just me and my mom when we sat at the end of one of the tables. Early into our meal, Layton reached us in her table rounds. She balanced her clip board on her hip and greeted us warmly.

"So what are you guys thinking in terms of riding today?" she asked. "We have three morning rides, an hour walking, but it's really steep, at 10, two hour-and-a-half backcountry walk/trot rides, one at 9:45 and one at 10:15, and lastly, a two hour all gaits going out at 9:30. What sounds good?" My mom looked over at me.

"Well, I'm going to be with Cade this morning so —"

"Rev, you can't just go with Cade every day," my mom cut in.

"Sure I can, he took this week off of wrangling," I explained.

"Mmhm, wow, how coincidental. I wonder why he choose this as his week off," Layton rolled her eyes.

"What I meant was," my mom said, looking at me, "You have to go on some rides with us, as a family. We did come here with an intention to spend some time together, you know."

"I know, it's just, Cade told me he would practice some gymkhana games with me this morning. Besides, Clay will be out with his age-group on a separate ride this morning anyway. How about we do a family ride this afternoon?"

"I can put you guys down for that . . ." Layton said, looking over her schedule, "One of our newer wranglers, Tristan, isn't assigned to a ride this afternoon. You could go out at three?"

"That's perfect!" I said. "And we'll have the breakfast ride too, we always do that. It's tomorrow right?"

"Yep, leaves at 7:30," Layton said. "And you're in luck, Dillon is leading it," she smiled.

"Really!" I said excitedly. "I was hoping she was still working here, but I haven't seen her; she wasn't at the campfire or anything."

"Yeah she had to go into town but she is still happily working here. I don't think you have to worry about her going anywhere," Layton winked. "I'll write y'all down for this afternoon and tomorrow morning," she said, walking away.

"See mom? This is perfect!" I said, shoving the rest of my food down my throat. "I gotta go, but I'll be back by lunch," I said quickly, then rushing towards the door.

*   *   *

"Okay, so I'm gonna have you do the keyhole run a couple of times, make sure you and Grayling are transitioning together alright, then I'll set up a few barrels for you," Cade explained from the ground.

"Sounds good," I said, clicking for Grayling to move forward and bringing her to alignment with the front gate. I took note of Gallatin's presence as he stood, tied to the railing, a few yards to my left. Cade climbed his way to the top of the fence where he took a seat to overview the arena. I looked up from the saddle and locked my eyes on a circle of cones at the opposite end.

"Start out at a trot for your first time, then by next round you'll have a better feel for the distance and can build up to a faster speed."

I nodded and sat back, pressing my legs into Grayling's sides. We trotted gently down the center of the arena and straight into the cone circle where I leaned into a quick turn and pressed Grayling back towards the other side of the arena. I sat deep, tightened the reins and kissed the air sending Grayling loping until we got in front of the gate. We made an abrupt stop, with only a few feet to spare; I looked up smiling, to see Cade staring back at me, arms crossed.

"I told you, to start with a trot," he said.

"Technically, I did start with a trot," I remarked. "I just didn't keep it there." Cade bit back a smile.

"Go again," he said. I continued with the keyhole exercise for a few more rounds, each time gaining speed, and simultaneously working on control. After a while, Cade hopped off the fence and pulled barrels out from the corners, using them to create a triangle pattern in the center of the arena.

"Remember, circle outside the right then cross to the left, then to the back point, always making a crazy-eight pattern between barrels. Trot it *all* the way through, the first time," he gave me a stern look. "*Then*, you can go into a lope, a controlled lope, should I say."

"Yes sir," I rolled my eyes. I went through the pattern a few times as he instructed, picking up the lope a couple times in.

"Not bad, but you're circling too wide, you need to narrow in and stay tight to the barrel."

"Yeah well, that's a little easier at a trot than at a lope," I said.

"It seems easier cause a trot is slower, but in reality, the movement of the horses' legs during the lope is better suited for circles and turns as they already have that natural inner curve to their body while they run, where in comparison, the momentum of the trot is straight forward." I stared at him blankly, reins loose, hands resting on the horn.

"I'll show you," Cade laughed. He swung off the fence and walked over to where Gallatin stood, untying his lead, looping the loose end over his neck and tying it next to where the other was clipped on the bottom ring of the halter. Cade laced the lead through his fingers, rested his left palm on Gallatin's shoulder and threw the rest of his body over, landing smoothly into a perfect seat. He lifted the reins and clucked, bringing Gallatin to a jog. He began forming a circle around the space where I stood, asking me to watch Gallatin's feet at various paces.

"Now, look up and watch his shoulders and his neck," he requested, repeating the same circle pattern.

"See the way he faces forward at the trot, even when I'm trying to turn him? Now watch for the difference." He sat back and sent Gallatin into a lope. "His neck is arched here, he's holding himself with his nose directed inward. That means a lot of his body weight is already set there, perfect for when you go into a turn."

"Now watch with the barrels," he said, slowing back to a trot. He stayed at a trot for his first time around, calling out directions with each movement. Coming back a second time, he loped off, loosely circling each barrel, then repeating a third time with tighter circles, to show how greatly they differentiate in speed.

"See what I mean?" Cade asked, trotting towards me. "And bareback no less," he smirked.

"Well that's not fair, you live here and Gallatin's your horse, so you're used to each other, you ride him all the time."

"Okay, I haven't been on Gray here since I was five, want me to ride her through it instead?" he asked with a cocky eyebrow raise.

"No, I would actually rather not see you do that. It would be too embarrassing," I said, "For you!" I called over my shoulder as I lead Grayling in the opposite direction.

"Right," he said, "That's the problem."

I took Grayling straight onto the course, taking the barrels one by one, trying hard to make smaller circles. I loped back to the start, knowing I had cut a few seconds off my time. I was expecting praise.

"That's better," he said, "But you're still forcing it too much."

"I don't know what that means!" I complained.

"Follow me," Cade motioned me over. We trotted side-by-side along the railing until we reached the final cone, where Cade began to circle.

"For starters, don't focus so much on your speed. And by that, I don't mean trot versus lope, I mean speed degrees within your loping, you don't need to worry about that, it'll pan out on its own," he said, transitioning in and out of loping patterns every few yards in a tight circle surrounding me. He sat deep on Gallatin's back, heels down, lead rope loosely hanging from his left hand.

"Give Grayling a little more credit," Cade started again. "She knows what she's doing, she's an old ranch horse, been playing these kinds of games since we broke her. You don't need to give so much direction with your reins."

"Okay, so what am I supposed to do instead?" I asked.

"To turn in a lope, all you have to do is lean into it, don't get all technical and overthink it, riding should feel natural, your biggest tool is your own body weight, use it," he told me. After he finished a few more circles, we made our way back towards the front of the arena.

"This is good practice for you, get to a point where you're comfortable doing just about anything on a horse and you'll be the one leading rides soon," he said. I laughed and looked at the ground.

"What next?" I asked.

"Your turn," he smiled, nodding ahead at the barrels. I bit my lip as I brought Grayling in front of Gallatin and straightened out to do the same circuit once again.

"Take a deep breath, let your body sink and meld to the saddle," I heard Cade say from behind me. I did as he instructed and paused there for a minute before starting my run.

Grayling transitioned smoothly into her lope, a pace I was able to maintain for the whole of the round. We kept a tight circle around the first barrel and charged towards the second with little hesitation. Bending around it and heading towards the back I remembered what Cade had said and found myself working to hold my center of gravity. Coming around the edge of the last barrel, I sat back and loosened the reins, allowing Gray to gallop freely back to the start. I smiled at Cade as we halted directly in front of him.

"Well done," he said, "That was really well done."

8

String lights shone against the night sky, highlighting the crowded open-wall structure that stood next to the horseshoe pit. Honky-tonk music drifted out from the inside where a three-part band played on a make-shift stage. I smoothed down the bottom of my ruffled, dusty-rose skirt and pulled my slouchy, beige, lace shirt back over the top of my shoulder. My parents walked hand in hand beside me while Clay ran ahead to meet his friends as soon as we got close.

Together, the three of us stepped onto the concrete floor of the structure and looked around. The sides were crowded with groups hanging over their drinks on the bar tables, the space in front of the band had a group of ten or so, line-dancing to Alan Jackson. Then in the back, lawn games were being played by people of all ages, including Clay and his friends.

I saw Cade across the way and smiled, giving a half wave, he smiled back before continuing his conversation with one of the other wranglers. My parents and I stood off to the side for a few minutes talking while a few more songs cycled and the line-dancing continued.

There was a sudden change in melody and the dance floor cleared, couples started taking up space on the floor as the songs got slower. My parents looked at each other, and I urged them on,

"Go," I said, giving them a little push in the back. "I haven't seen you guys swing dance in years, get out there, have fun," I smiled. My mom smiled and touched my shoulder before taking my dad's arm, as they walked to the center of the floor. I ran a strand of hair behind my ear and watched the couples spin around each other as the band covered George Strait's "I Just Want to Dance with You." They looked so happy and effortless.

I felt a tap on my shoulder, and before I could turn, was being pulled by my elbow onto the dance floor. Within seconds I found myself standing in front of Cade as he took both my hands and began taking me side to side. He dipped me gently and followed it with a double spin. It took me a few steps to keep from stumbling and stepping on his toes.

"I'm a little out of practice," I said, when he pulled me in.

"Glad to hear that," he smiled. "I'd be very offended if I found out you had a swing dance partner back home."

"Afraid not," I smirked as we continued going around the floor. Another swing song followed and we kept on without stopping. I wouldn't have noticed the song changes at all if it weren't for us being the last ones on the floor a few minutes later, as the rest had cleared with the faster tempo. Cade and I looked at each other and smiled, backing away from the floor and stepping into the cool air for a minute.

"I forgot how fun that was," I said, moving my hair to one side as I leaned against one of the posts.

"I didn't," Cade said, giving me a quick smile. I looked at him before turning away and looking across to the opposite end of the structure. I shook my head, seeing my parents chatting with other parents and couples and knowing that Clay would remain with his group for the rest of the night as always.

"You know, every year I'm the only one who leaves this ranch without new friends," I said.

"Well, I'm just so good that you never want any new ones," Cade said. I laughed and smiled at the ground,

"That's valid," I said. We stood there for a few minutes not saying anything as the sound of guitars and soft voices filled the air. A new beat started up and the lead singer began calling out directions. It was time for the square dance.

"Shall we?" I looked at Cade.

"Let's go," he said, and we ran onto the floor to join the others. Small circles formed and we all grabbed hands with our neighbors. As the fiddle played, there were partner spins, group dances and plenty of boot stomps. Direction after direction we all tried and laughed and danced as the stars grew brighter.

9

"As we pass through this creek, if you look down the bank to the right, you'll see the beginning of Calgry Meadow, a spot very popular among gangs of elk," Dillon said from the front of the line. My mom was behind her, then my dad, and lastly, me and Clay. Behind us, a few more ranch guests followed, including another family, and then a second wrangler took up the rear. I breathed deep and closed my eyes as the breeze tugged at my hair. I could feel the warmth of the sun as it continued rising until the entire sky was lit.

"Rev look!" I heard Clay say from behind me.

"What?" I turned back and followed his finger until I found what he was pointing at. A beautiful brown elk cow stood protectively between us and her newborn baby. I smiled as I saw the baby nuzzle at its mom's chest. Elk are often dangerous when their calves are that young but I knew we were far enough away that there wasn't any big concern. Even with that, however, I encouraged Clay to remain quiet and watched the elk subtly, refraining from making any eye-contact. Our line of horses continued along but before we were completely out of sight I realized there was a second baby lying in the grass next to its brother.

It wasn't long before we reached the cookout spot. One by one we got off our horses and tied them along the hitching rail before getting in line for food and finding seats by the fire pit. I looked around at all the faces, still confused why Cade wasn't one of them; he never missed a breakfast ride. Dillon sat next to me and starting asking about school and future plans.

"Rev is going to Duke," my dad answered for me.

"She officially signs the papers soon after we get home and leaves the day after graduation. She is in the honors program after all," my mom added proudly.

"Wow," Dillon said. "That's incredible, congratulations Rev." I smiled and thanked her before abruptly changing the subject. It didn't take long for Clay to stand up in front of everyone and begin another storytelling session. I smirked and rolled my eyes at my parents who laughed with me at the familiarity of the situation.

After finishing my plate, I got up to take it to the trash and collided with Dillon who was up grabbing a second bread roll. She looked at me and nodded her head to the side, leading me a few feet further from the rest of the group.

"So, you don't seem quite at the same level of happiness as your parents," Dillon remarked.

"What do you mean?" I asked.

"About Duke," she said.

"Oh, that," I bit my lip. "It's not that I'm not happy. I am, and I worked really hard for it and it's gonna be great. I just," I stuttered, "Being here, being at the ranch, riding, being with these people again." I looked at the ground, "I guess I'm just not ready to go back to reality yet," I said. "I don't want to think about it."

"Then you shouldn't," Dillon said, putting her arm around my shoulder. "You deserve to relax and enjoy your time here, in our little slice of heaven," she smiled, looking up at the beautiful blue sky.

"Thanks," I said; she nodded and walked back to her seat.

*   *   *

When we got back to the ranch I immediately peeled off from my family and made my way to the arena, where I had seen Cade lunging a horse as we got off our own horses in the barn. As Dillon and a few other wranglers began untacking horses and releasing them to the pasture, the rest of the riders quickly dispersed from the area, leaving it so that the only noise was the sound of hoof beats. When I reached the railing, Cade had his back turned to me, so I made a point of being extra loud.

"Hey! Where were you? I thought you were going on the ride with us?" I saw his back tense up at my voice, but he remained standing there, without responding or even turning around.

"Um, Cade?" I said. "Hello?" I asked, crawling through the railing and stepping into the arena. He gave the horse the signal to stop and starting pulling in the slack on the rope.

"You're not supposed to come in the arena when someone's working a horse. It isn't safe," he said stiffly, walking the horse to the railing, undoing its lead line and clipping the hanging rope to its halter.

"Sorry, I just--" I stumbled, surprised by his response. "Is everything okay?" I asked. He made eye contact with me for the first time and held it there for a minute, obvious anger growing.

"You're going to Duke?" he asked, but it didn't sound like a question.

"Who told you that?" I asked.

"That's not an answer," he said with frustration.

"Yes . . ." I answered slowly, "Yes I am."

"Shit, Rev . . . what the hell? And why the hell are you going?"

"What do you mean why am I going? It's one of the top schools in the country!" I said defensively.

"That's not what I'm talking about and you know it," he said. I looked at the ground, not knowing what to say.

"Were you ever planning on telling me?" he asked.

"Yes, of course . . . eventually, just not yet," I said, evasively.

"When?"

"I don't know! Probably when I signed the papers," I admitted.

"A month from now when you're back home and don't have to face me," he said, scoffing under his breath.

"I'm sorry. I'm going to Duke. I couldn't look at you and say that," I said.

"You know why you couldn't look at me and say that? Because you're afraid of the truth, you're afraid of why you're doing it, and you know that I would be the one to point it out," he said, looking me straight in the eye.

"Maybe I didn't want to freaking tell you because I knew how much you were going to criticize me! If you're my friend, if you care about me, then you'll support me in this, you should want me to do what is going to make me happy!" I said with exasperation.

"I do care about you, and me wanting you to be happy is exactly why I'm pissed that you're doing this," he said.

"You don't know what the hell you're talking about Cade," I said.

"I don't?"

"No, you don't, and you have no right to criticize my life decisions. We were friends when we were kids, I don't owe you anything. What I owe is to myself, to do what's best for me. I made this choice and I'm happy with it. I'm thrilled, I can't wait, because this is the choice that will take me somewhere in life. I have no regrets, no worries, no concerns. These are going to be the best four years of my life. There is *nothing* I would rather be doing," I said, arms crossed.

"I know you better than that, Rev," Cade said.

"No, you don't, Cade, you *used* to know me," I said coldly.

"Don't get all high and mighty and act like you've changed. People don't really change, not unless they force it. You're the most yourself when you're a kid, before you start pretending to be things you're not." I wouldn't look at him, tears welled in my eyes but I refused to let them out.

"What happened?" he asked. "Why are you pretending? What happened to the Rev that wore her hair in braids and didn't care what other people thought and who lived for the weeks she got to spend on this ranch?" he asked.

"She changed, she grew up and she's happier now," I said, pretending his words weren't killing me.

"Come on, Rev, there's a reason you're back," he said.

"Yes, and that reason being my parents bought some plane tickets. I was never planning on coming back," I said, trying to convince myself that was true.

"Since when?" he asked.

"Since I realized this world was distracting me from my real life," I said, looking at him again.

"Working with animals, doing stuff with your hands, being around good wholesome people, appreciating nature for what it is. Life doesn't get more real than this, Rev," Cade said.

"It's not enough," I said. "This isn't the kind of life I want," I lied. "There's more out there, better things out there, and that's where I'm headed." Cade nodded his head repetitively at the ground, face flushed, and eyes watery. He looked back up and started walking past me. He paused for a second at my shoulder, looking at me blindly.

"Screw you," he said, before leaving the arena altogether. I looked after him and put my hand up to my mouth. I couldn't hold it back any longer and my tears were streaming. I fell to my knees and buried my face in my hands as puffs of dust surrounded me.

10

Shutting the door behind me, I tightened the strings of my hoodie and let the oversized sleeves hang loosely over my hands. My hair was a tangled mess and my cheeks were still flushed from the exhaustion of tears. I walked hurriedly away from the cabin, plowing down the grasses beneath my boots and heading towards the lower gravel path. As I came upon the outer lodge area, I saw that my parents were out on the deck with some other couples, sipping on cocktails. I kept my head down hoping they wouldn't notice, but it only took a moment for my mom to look up and call over to me.

"Rev! Where you headed? Come over with us!" she said, motioning with her arm.

"I was just gonna go down to the barn. I wanted to see all the horses out in pasture, before it's too dark," I told her.

"Well, be fast, campfire's starting soon, we were all about to head down," she said.

"Not tonight, mom," I said. "Not really in the mood and I'm pretty tired, but you guys have fun, I'll see you after." My mom looked like she wanted to question and say more but I turned around before she could.

By the time I reached the barn, the sun was already starting to set, and the soft light of dusk cast a glow over everything in sight, making it that much more beautiful. I walked down to the pasture gate and climbed up, taking a seat on the top railing. I heard shuffling behind me and turned to see that Cade had walked up from the other side of the barn.

"I, I didn't go to the campfire, so that I wouldn't run into you," I said quietly.

"Yeah, me too," Cade said. "Maybe you shouldn't have picked the spot I spend the most time at."

"Look, Cade, I'm sorry. I mean it. I should have told you, but it's not like I did it on purpose to hurt you, and I feel like you're acting like I did," I said, still on the railing, but having flipped my body around to face him.

"It's not even the fact you didn't tell me. Yes, that pisses me off and yes, it pisses me off that you're lying about why you're doing it, but that's sadness and anger. What hurt was hearing you go on about how there are better things out there and this life isn't enough for you. It's not the first time I've heard that, Rev," Cade said, flares of anger and pain in his eyes. "Does my mom ring a bell?"

I looked at the ground, realizing what I'd done.

"She said she loved it, and us, she was happy, until she wasn't, and she left with just a note, telling us why it wasn't good enough here." He looked away, and I could see his eyes reddening from forming tears.

"Cade, I---"

"Save it," he snapped back. "Don't act like you forgot or didn't know. I'm the one who found the note and I came to you right away. You've known the whole time."

"And do you remember what I said, what I said when you told me?" I asked, Cade looked up. "I said that I couldn't believe anyone could take a place like this for granted, but more than that I couldn't believe anyone could take a family like yours for granted. And I hate that it looks like I am," I said, head bowing down.

"Your mom," I jumped off the rail and took his hand, "She was such an incredibly lucky woman. She was lucky to live here, she was lucky to be married to your dad, and she was lucky to have wonderful children and she was especially lucky to have a son as wonderful as you." I looked at him deliberately. "And I'm just as lucky. Lucky to spend time in a place like this, lucky to know these kinds of people, and so lucky to have you as a friend." Cade wouldn't look up but I saw him bite his lip. "And I shouldn't take that for granted."

There was silence for a few moments, just the tug of the breeze, pulling my hair out from the hood of my sweatshirt. Cade stepped back and walked a few paces to my right, so that he was in front of the pasture, gazing out at the grasses and trees as the sky lost its last light. The air was quickly growing colder and I could smell the burning embers of the campfire back up the main path. Cade leaned his forehead on the top rail and pressed the ball of his foot on a rock below. I let a few minutes pass before walking up beside him.

"Cade, I'm sorry for what I said earlier and how I said it, I wasn't thinking, but I mean what I just said. I meant it when I first said it, six years ago, and I mean it now, more than anything else I've said to you since I got here."

He didn't answer right away, just kept looking thoughtfully at the ground. I then saw his eyes flicker as he lifted his head and gazed back out in front of him.

"I just know how grateful I am to have this as my home," he said. "While other people are always looking for the new thing to keep them happy, they seem to forget the minimal, everyday things, that really keep them happy at core. If you can remember those, I'm not saying you'll be happy all the time, but at least then you have the peace of knowing where your heart is. My mom never had that."

I felt myself mindlessly racking my brain, wondering if I really knew the things that were closest to my own heart. I then realized that I was going about it all wrong, the overthinking of everything is exactly what clouds us from realizing those things at our core.

"*We can only be said to be alive in those moments when our hearts are conscious of our treasures*," I said under my breath.

"I thought I was the one who handed out random quotes of wisdom?" Cade said, starting to turn back to look at me.

"It's a Thornton Wilder quote," I explained, "He's the author of *Our Town*, a play I read for school."

"Oh," Cade said. "It seemed a little too eloquent for you," he winked, with the first glimpse of a real smile.

"Shut up!" I laughed, pushing him to the side. He grabbed my arm but instead of pushing me back, just pulled me into a hug. I held tight and looked up at him, resting my chin vertically on his chest.

"Do you want to talk about it?" I asked him.

"Talk about what?" he asked, staring blankly ahead.

"You know what," I said. "Earlier."

"Not right now," he said. We stood there for a few moments before he dropped my arms gingerly and we began wandering under the barn overhang. As we came around the corner to a spot outside the work shed, Cade stopped in his tracks and bent down, reaching his hand into the dirt.

"What are you doing?" I laughed.

"Hold out your wrist," he said, standing up, covering something in his palm. I rolled my eyes and held my hand out. He pushed a thin band of metal over my folded hand and onto my wrist. I looked down then back up at him curiously as he left his hand there, holding mine.

"It's a piece of scrap metal," I said.

"It's metaphor," Cade said. "It's a circle, it's forever," he cleared his throat. "It's the little things, conscious of our treasures, right?"

"Right," I said slowly, avoiding eye contact. I fiddled with it on my wrist for a minute, passing the time, but I could feel his eyes watching me.

"How about we go join the campfire?" I asked, finally looking at him. "You can entertain people with your 'exaggerated' stories again?" I smiled.

"Yeah," he laughed. "Let's go," he said, poking my arm as we started walking, "I bet I can eat more s'mores than you," he said.

"No way," I said.

"Yep, and cook them to perfection faster and cook more on each stick, without dropping a single one," he puffed out his chest.

"Oh, we'll see about that."

11

I woke up to the familiar pattern of taps at my window.

"Morning Cade," I said, opening the window and turning to look at the time. The wall clock was framed with a lasso and the hands were legs kicking their boots up in the air.

"It's five in the morning, what are you doing here?"

"Thought you might wanna help with the round up," he smiled.

"Give me two minutes," I said, running in the other room to change.

When we got down to the barn, Dillon and Tripp were already tacking up the last horses.

"Wait, but who will I ride?" I asked. "Grayling isn't one of the overnight horses."

"I told Jake to sleep in, so you can ride his horse, Daze shouldn't give you any trouble," Cade assured me.

"And before you ask how I knew you were gonna come, you've been asking about the round up since you were nine, there was no way you weren't gonna jump at the chance," he said.

"Fair enough," I laughed.

"Rev my darling, here's your girl for the day," Dillon said, walking over a beautiful dun mare. "And here's your walkie," she had me turn to the side so she could clip it on my belt.

"Thank you," I said, taking the reins and moving to put my foot in the stirrup. Dillon hoped on a nearby horse and stood with me as Cade walked back to get Gallatin.

"So, should I be nervous?" I asked.

"You don't have to worry," Dillon said. "It can be dangerous if you're not paying attention, that's how you get yourself caught in a stampede. But as long as you listen to us and follow our instructions, you'll be fine. They're ranch horses; they do this same routine every day."

"Ready to go?" Cade called out. I looked up to see him and Tripp at the head of the path, waving us over. Dillon and I trotted to meet them. Once all together, we made a quick turn to the left and headed east through the day pasture. Long grasses and wildflowers reached up to our heels, tickling the horse's sides as we made our way to the far gate.

Cade reached down to unhook the latch and let the rusty metal clang against itself as it swung open. We all crept through together, taking our first steps into the open grassland that is the night pasture.

"I'll cover the back," Tripp said. "Cade take Rev around the front to get them going and then do a perimeter to gather strays. Dillon can go around the sides and help me get them through the gate."

"Okay," Cade said. Then turning to me, "Let's go." He started Gallatin at a jog and I trotted up to ride next to him.

"So what's happening here?"

"Just follow my lead," Cade said. A large group of horses were gathered up ahead, grazing by a creek bed.

"Here we go," Cade said, then turning immediately into a lope. I followed suit as he made a wide half circle to the right of the herd. As we loped around the back a couple of horses started running, then enticing the entire herd into frenzy, galloping mindlessly towards the gate.

"Same thing every morning," Cade said. "They act like we're a pack of wolves until they see the gates open and then they're happy to run towards breakfast."

"Do we follow them?" I asked.

"No," Cade said. "Dillon and Tripp are going to circle them up and guide as they get close to the gate. But that was just the main group, now we have to ride around the rest of the pastureland searching for strays until Tripp lets us know that they have them all."

We continued on through the grasses until we came across a wooded back area, forcing me to leave Cade's side and walk behind him as we began weaving in and out of trees and boulders.

"The last few years on the ranch have been good," Cade said. "I mean homeschooling always made it easy to spend most of my time working, but right after you were here last, I turned 16 which made me eligible to test out of school for good. So for the past three and a half years now, I've been full time working, doing shoeing, wrangling, overall ranch-hand stuff, helping my dad out. It's been great. With Tripp working side by side with our dad, Layton doing customer service and me on my way to being Head Wrangler, it's a family business through and through. It's been one since my grandpa bought this ranch in the 50's and we're gonna make sure it stays a family business going into the future. It's our way of life, you know? I wouldn't ask for anything different."

We ambled along slowly as I offered updates on the past few years of my life. Talking to Cade always made me think about how different our upbringings had been. In my hometown, they're so focused on school, careers, material success, they make you feel like there's only one path in life, but there are a million different paths to suit a million different people. You just have to figure out what things in your life mean enough to dedicate to.

"Look up there," Cade said, pulling out a Walkie Talkie. He pointed up ahead at two horses, one silver and the other dun. "Tripp, I've got an eye on Jem and Midge at the south end of the pasture, I'll rope them and bring them over to you now." The radio buzz sounded off and Cade reached around to strap it back on his belt.

"Okay," he said. "I'm gonna grab these two and take them over to Tripp, you can keep looking in this back area and radio me if there's anything urgent."

Cade adjusted the grip on his reins and jogged slowly towards the horses, untying the rope from the side of his saddle. He looped slip knots around each horse's neck and held the rope ends loosely in his free hand. They stayed obediently at his side, keeping exact pace with each other's hoof beats, as he jogged past me on Gallatin.

"I shouldn't be long," Cade called over his shoulder.

I breathed deeply, sinking down into the saddle, unsure of where to go. A soft breeze picked up and blew thin strands of hair across my face. I huddled deeper into my flannel, wishing I'd brought a real jacket. Pressing my legs into Daze's sides, I made my way across the last stretch to the end of the pasture, where I began rounding the perimeter.

As I came under the corner of some trees and back into an open area, I noticed a large lump in the grasses up ahead but the morning fog was too dense for me to see clearly. I rode up closer cautiously, and saw that it was one of the ranch horses. I got off Daze and tied her to a tree, then walked up slowly to where the horse was lying. Hands shaking, I pulled my Walkie Talkie out and radioed over to the others,

"Guys, I, uh, I found a horse. It's a bay mare. I'm afraid something might be wrong with her, she's breathing really deeply and it looks like there's a sticky yellow liquid on her side. I don't know what to do, she hasn't even looked up since I came over here," I rambled on, terrified that I wouldn't be able to help.

"Where are you?" I heard Cade ask back.

"I don't know, I went to the very back where the fence is, and then I came in a little bit to a small clearing and--"

"Okay, I know where you are, we'll be there in a minute," Tripp chimed in. I heard the radio buzz go off and I was left alone, shakily walking a few steps closer to the horse.

A few minutes had passed when I heard the gentle "whoa" command and the slowing of hoof beats. I turned to see Tripp, Dillon and Cade walking up behind me. Tripp slid off his horse first and handed his reins to Dillon, who slowly got off alongside Cade, and walked the horses over to the trees to get tied up. Cade pulled some more rope off the back of his saddle and walked over to join his brother, who was squatting beside the horse's head.

"It's Quartz," Tripp said, he rested his hand on her neck as she took heavy breaths. He leaned over and examined her side, where the yellowish liquid seemed to originate. "Looks like our girl has starting foaling," he looked back with a smile.

"That's early," Dillon commented; arms crossed.

"Yeah but not too early, shouldn't be a problem. Go ahead and give the vet a call though, I'd like to have him examine her, just to be on the safe side," Tripp said, moving back towards the horse's head and undoing the rope around his belt. "Give me a hand, would ya?" he asked. Dillon walked across and helped him loop the rope around the horse's neck. I looked at Cade, confused.

"Quartz is pregnant," he explained. "And 'foaling' is what we call one of the last stages of pregnancy." I watched as Tripp and Dillon encouraged Quartz up to her feet, she wavered slightly, but stood strong as soon as she was able to get her footing.

"I'm going to hand-walk her back to the barn. Dillon, Cade, if one of you could take Woody back for me?"

"No problem," Dillon said. "I'll call the vet on the way back." Tripp held Quartz' lead rope gingerly as they slowly made their way out of the clearing. With Cade and I jogging back to the barn side-by-side, Dillon followed us, trailing Tripp's horse, Woody, behind her own.

"So is it bad that Quartz was lying down? Like is that healthy and all?" I asked Cade.

"It's normal, encouraged actually, as long as she continues to get up and lie down repeatedly, she's just helping her foal get into the proper position for birth. We'll monitor it though; if she stays down for too long a period at once, it could be harmful. Now that she's so close to birth we'll probably have to start a new schedule so that we have a wrangler down in the barn at all hours."

12

"Hey!" I said, walking hurriedly up to a band of wranglers outside the barn.

"What'd the vet say? Is she going to be okay?" I asked, as soon as I had reached them.

"She should be fine," Tripp said. "Nothing's wrong, she's just a few weeks ahead of where we expected, horse pregnancies are typically around 11 months, so a matter of days isn't enough time in the long run to really make us concerned."

"It's just time to separate her from the rest of the remuda, and put her in her individual stall," Dillon told me. "And don't worry," she smiled. "We've already made up her stall, it's been ready for weeks, just waiting for her." Cade and I peeled off from the group as they began organizing plans and schedules for the rest of the week.

"So, you're sure she's fine?" I asked.

"Yeah, she's just early, that's all. Foaling is just a part of the process. She's in great health," he reassured me.

"Well I'm glad to hear that," I said. "Is there anything else I can help with?"

"Not unless you feel like doing chores with me," Cade laughed.

"Sure," I smiled. "Why not."

"Well in that case," Cade smiled, "We've got a lot of stalls to muck!" he moved to the side and grabbed two pitch forks that were leaning against the side of the barn.

"Oh joy," I said, grabbing one of the forks.

*   *   *

"Hey watch it!" I coughed, waving my arms at the dust as Cade rolled a wheelbarrow past me.

"What? You afraid of a little dirt?" he asked, setting the barrel down and grabbing a handful of shavings to toss in my direction.

"You really want to start that?" I ran to grab the shovel and threw a full scoop of shavings back at him. I was turning to get another when Cade tackled me by the waist and together we crash-landed into the full pile, flakes flying up and getting lost in our hair. I looked over to see his face turned up at the roof, balancing a flake on the ridge of his nose. I burst out laughing;

"That's a great look."

"You're not much better," he said, shaving the flakes off. I smiled, tracing my finger in the pile.

"Gallatin's been needing a bath." Cade looked at me, "Want to give me a hand?"

"Let's do it," I smiled, taking his hand as he pulled me up.

"Grab a bucket from the tack room and meet me by the rack." I did as he asked and started the hose running as soon as I arrived at the shower rack. Cade walked up and tied Gallatin to the post. He handed me the shampoo and I ran it through Gallatin's mane and tail, then rubbing it all along his body. Cade followed with the hose, washing down the suds.

"Hey, is there a scounge in that bucket?" Cade asked. "I want to get some of this excess water off."

"Let me check," I bent down and pulled out a long black piece of hard rubber with a metal end. "Is this it?" I stood up to show him, but he wasn't there. I turned, coming face to face with Cade as he sprayed me all over with the cold water. My tank top was completely drenched, revealing the pink and brown striped bikini top I was wearing underneath. Cade stepped back, laughing.

"Are you wearing a swimsuit?" he asked.

"Yes, I am," I said simply, ringing out my hair.

"Uh-huh, right, why?" Cade asked, raising a brow.

"Because I'm smart, and I knew this was gonna happen," I said, motioning to the dripping water. "You've done it every time I've ever helped you with chores. I came prepared."

"I'm impressed," he laughed. I took the opportunity to grab the hose from his hand and quickly turned the nozzle to spray him back.

"Holy shit, that's cold!" Cade yelled, putting his hands up to block his face. I turned the hose face down.

"Yeah, it is!" I said, lifting it to spray him one more time before turning it off.

"Well," Cade said, slicking water off his arms and looking over at me, "I feel like at this point we may as well just head to the creek." I smiled and clapped my hands excitedly.

"Yes!" I cheered.

* * *

"One . . ."

"Two . . ."

"Three!" Together we jumped off the bank and into the deep part of the creek. The water surged up and bubbled over my shoulders as I came up for air. The sun immediately began to beat down on my face and chest while I moved my hands up to slick back my hair.

"It feels so good!" I said.

"I know, this is the first time I've been in this season," Cade admitted. "The weather's finally warm enough."

"Man, I can't imagine passing this up," I said. "It would be so cool to be this close to a river. If I lived here, I'd be in every day!" I said, falling backwards into the water.

"Says the girl who's never experienced a Montana winter," Cade smirked. I shrugged, laughing and squeezing the water from the ends of my hair.

"Someday," I said.

13

"Two fours," I said.

"B.S.," Clay said.

"Ugh, how do you always know?" I reached across the table to pull the stack of cards over and add them to my hand.

"Three fives," my mom said.

"B.S.," I said.

"I would say take them, but you already did," my mom said, handing me her three cards with a cocky smile.

"One six," my dad said.

"Two sevens," Clay said before looking over at my dad, who sat back in the couch with his arms crossed.

"Wait, was that your last card?" Clay asked.

"Yup," my dad said, taking a sip of his drink.

"Every time," Clay said, slapping his cards on the table. I rubbed my hands on my denim-clad thighs and stood up to stretch, my slouchy ombre top falling over the edge of my shoulder.

"Well, I'm gonna go get a cookie from the lodge, anyone else want one?" I asked, heading towards the door. They all murmured and shook their heads "no" as I left the room.

When I got to the lodge, the lights were on and the outside door was open, but it was otherwise empty. I reached into the jar on the front table and pulled out a snickerdoodle. As I went to take my first bite, I felt something touch my other hand, and before I knew it, I was spun in a circle and dipped to the ground. I looked up to see Cade's smirking face.

"Hey," he said, pulling me upright.

"Smooth," I laughed, taking another bite. "Where did you come from?"

"I was out on the porch," he said. "I'm surprised you didn't hear my boots coming in."

"I'm not," I said. "I was much too focused on my cookie," I smiled. He laughed.

"You got any plans for the rest of your night?" he asked.

"Not unless I want to play more BS with my family, which is a definite no," I grit my teeth. "So, what have you got in mind?"

"Well, I seem to remember, years ago, a certain horseshoe challenge from off the top of the roof, and I'm still up for a rematch. That is, unless you're afraid you've lost your touch," he smiled.

"I guess four years later it's about time we got to that rematch . . ." I looked over my shoulder. "Let's go!" I said, motioning with my hand.

Together we walked around the outside of the lodge, around the swing set and seesaw, made a stop at the pit to pick up our horseshoes, and then on to the barn-dance awning. Cade gave me a lift on to the outer banister and from there I was able to scoot up and over. He followed suit and we walked to the opposite edge, facing the pit.

"Ladies first," he said, backing away and spreading his hands.

"How very kind," I laughed, moving my arm back to take the first throw. My horseshoe landed horribly array, a good ten feet in from the pit. I saw Cade bite his lip back, trying not to laugh.

"Alright hot shot, let's see you do it," I said. He stepped forward with confidence and tossed his horseshoe expertly, leaving it in the dust just to the left of the post. He turned back and gave a dramatic bow.

"Well you've had four years to practice," I said.

"You caught me. This is where I spent all my free time, preparing for this moment," he said sarcastically.

"Don't act like that's far off base," I said. He laughed, throwing his hands up in defense. I stepped forward and aimed hard, landing my second throw almost as close as Cade's. I turned around and finished with an even-more dramatic curtsy. We went on like that for three games until Cade managed to land one perfectly around the post, I swallowed my pride and admitted him winner. He smiled broadly and dusted off his shoulders as I crossed my arms over my own, rubbing along the goosebumps.

"You're shivering," he said, then taking off his jacket, "Here."

"You don't have to," I said.

"I do if I don't want you to be cold."

"I guess that's true," I smiled, pulling it over my shoulders. We sat down on the edge and watched the stars speckle all across Montana's famously big sky. I looked down at my wrist where I noticed the hand on my watch ticking quickly towards 12.

"Oh, wow, it's a lot later than a thought," I said, starting to stand back up. "I should really head back to my cabin. You need to get some sleep."

"And why is that?" he asked me, head cocked to the side.

"You're the one who has to be ready to help with the round-up in like, five hours."

"So?"

"So, you need sleep. I know you're already tired and you'll be exhausted all day tomorrow if you don't go to bed now."

"I'm okay with missing sleep when it means being tired with you," he smiled, patting the ground next to him. "Come on, we'll go in soon, just a little longer." I rolled my eyes at the cliché.

"Five more minutes," I agreed. "That's it."

"Yeah, you keep thinking that," Cade said, prodding my arm. I laughed and gazed back up at the sky. The North Star was immediately in front of us, shining bright in all its glory. My eyes caught sight of my watch again; it had inched past midnight, making it officially Friday, my last full day at the ranch.

"I can't believe that after all these years, I'm finally back here, and in less than two days, I have to leave again," I said, leaning my head on my knees and pulling the sleeves of the sweatshirt over my hands.

"Don't think about it," Cade said. "I'm trying hard not to," he added. I looked over at him but he was staring straight ahead, avoiding my eyes. A few wordless moments passed with only the distant whinnies of horses in pasture as background noise but I could tell there was something Cade wanted to say.

"What are you thinking about?" I asked. He took a long pause before answering.

"You know, I can't think of a single time before where you wouldn't tell me what you wished for," he said softly. "Usually I didn't even have to ask, it was just expected that we'd tell each other. What's big enough to break that?"

This time I was the one staring forward. I felt Cade's eyes on me, waiting for a response. I took a long time to respond, sitting there, trying to take in deep, slow breaths.

"I wished for an answer. I wished for clarity. I wished for my mind and heart to stop conflicting," I said finally, biting my lip in regret immediately after. I refused to look at him, just tilted my head upward and busied myself trying to find constellations. Moments later, a long, flashing light, crossed in front of us, a shooting star. I looked down in my lap and almost laughed at the irony.

"Make a wish," I said, batting my eyelashes to keep the tears from falling.

"I did," Cade said simply.

"Yeah? What'd you wish for?" I asked, not really expecting an answer, but looking back at him for the first time.

"This," he said, leaning forward and pressing his lips into mine. It was soft and sweet and yet I felt myself getting lost in it. I wasn't thinking, just giving in to the natural sensation, it felt completely different from when I had kissed Mitt. But when our lips unlocked and I looked into his eyes, I immediately shied away. I turned my face away from him as all my thoughts and worries came back to me.

"Rev--" Cade started.

"I have to get back," I said quickly taking off his jacket and handing it back to him. "You should to," I said, still not looking at him, and rushing to climb back off the roof. He might have said more, but I didn't hear him, as soon as I hit the ground I hurried back to my cabin, with no intention of looking back.

14

I was restless all night, tossing and turning, never sleeping more than twenty minutes at a time. At one point, I looked over at my clock and saw that it was just past 4:30. They wouldn't start the round-up for another hour so no one would be at the barn yet if I hurried. I grabbed my heaviest jacket from the closet, and pulled my boots on over the jeans I was still wearing from last night. I climbed out the window and hustled down to the barn, feeling my way through the dark. When I got there, I breathed a sigh of relief to see Daze was one of the round-up horses again this morning. I tacked up quickly and headed on to the trail.

The air was cool and the first light was just starting to show when I reached the ridge. Sage grasses dominated the area; I had to step back towards the trail in order to find a tree suited for tying Daze. I started walking back from the trees when I noticed a strange figure in the grasses. I tilted my head curiously when I noticed a second figure behind it, a larger black blur near the trees on the opposite side. The smaller figure turned in my direction and I locked eyes with Cade.

"I see you still know your way here," he said, turning his back to me. I took a breath and sat next to him, leaving a few feet in between.

"How could I forget?" I said softly.

"I don't know but it sure seems like you tried to forget this place," he said, looking at me. I looked down and fiddled the flower buds in my hands.

"You know," Cade continued, "You're not supposed to ride off without telling a wrangler, even if you do know your way around, and you're *especially* not supposed to take a wrangler's horse."

"How did you know I was going to come here?" I asked, after a pause.

"Because, whether you want to admit it or not, I know you, Rev," Cade said irritably.

"We have to talk," he said.

"There's nothing to talk about, you were caught up in the moment, that's all," I said hurriedly.

"No I wasn't," he said deliberately. "And you weren't either."

"Cade stop," I begged.

"Why?" he said with underlying anger.

"Because there's no point!" I said, looking at him for the first time, with tears forming in the corners of my eyes. "It's not gonna happen, it's not gonna work, we lead two different lives that don't fit together, in two different places that really don't fit together, so there's no point! Just stop," I said, shoving my face in my hands as I could no longer stop the tears.

"You know what, Rev?" I lifted my head slightly. "Go back to your life, go to your east coast school, be a legacy, spend every day worried about money and success and status and whatever other crap you pretend to care about. Go live whatever freaking life that is, I'm not going to keep trying to get you to listen to your heart," he said, getting off the ground and holding up his hands, "I'm done." He walked straight to Gallatin, swung his leg over and took off at a gallop, never turning to look back at me.

Watching him leave made me feel like I had lost a part of myself, the best part of myself, the part of me that was free and fearless and honest and happy. I pulled the photo from my pocket as my tears turned into sobs. The sun had just risen and yet I'd never felt so surrounded by darkness.

15

"Rev, you said you were going to the lodge for a minute and coming right back, you were gone for hours! I finally get some sleep in the middle of night when I hear you come in, then I wake up the next morning to find you gone again! Now this is unacceptable, and I am waiting for an explanation," my mom's face was dead serious as she crossed her arms tighter.

"I'm sorry," I said, letting hair fall in front of my face, hoping it would hide my puffy cheeks.

"Sorry isn't an explanation."

"Well, then I don't have one," I said, trying to brush past her.

"Rev," she put her arm on my shoulder, "What is going on?" When I didn't answer, she turned me to face her and caught sight of my heavy, red-streaked eyes. "Have you been crying? What happened?" I put my face in my hands and took a deep breath.

"Answer me!" she said, losing concern and going back to frustration.

"Nothing, I'm fine, I just--" I stuttered trying to catch my words. "Please," I begged, "I don't want to talk about it right now. I can't talk about it right now, so please can you just send me to my room for the day or something?" I said, my eyes growing heavy with water once again. She watched me deliberately and bit her lip, weighing how to feel.

"Fine," she said after a while. "Go to your room," she said, "But when I say we will talk in a few hours, I mean it." She looked at me sternly. I nodded and made my way down the hall, holding back my tears until the door was closed and I fell onto the bed, covering my weeping with blankets.

*   *   *

I heard a knock on my door as I lay weeping against my pillows, but before I could find the energy to get up or even say anything, it swung open. My mom stood in the doorway, the stern look on her face somewhat dissolving when she took notice of my state. She shut the door behind her and sat at the foot of my bed, waiting for me to say something.

"I'm sorry mom," I said, after a while.

"I know you are," she said. "But that still doesn't explain anything."

"I fought with Cade, okay? Badly, but please don't make me go through the details. Talking about it won't help and neither will be thinking about it, which is what I'm already drowning myself with," I said, flopping back on my pillows.

"I'm sorry you guys fought, you've been friends for so long, I know that must hurt, but don't you think you're overreacting? I'm sure it will resolve soon, no reason to coop yourself up in here all miserable." I put my face in my hands, sniffling, and trying to calm my breathing.

"I'd really just like to be alone," I said meekly.

"Fine," my mom said, standing up angrily, "Ruin our last trip with you, go right ahead." As she left and slammed the door, I felt the aching in my heart grow stronger. Was she right? Was it all my fault?

*　　*　　*

"It's the final night hoedown!" my dad said, as my whole family ambushed me. "They're teaching some new line dances. Come on, Rev, you have to go!"

"Yeah, don't be a loser," Clay said.

"It is your last night here." My mom finally said something.

"Who knows when or if we'll be back," my dad added. I sucked in air, trying to pretend like I hadn't heard that.

"I don't want any stress in the morning. I'm just going to get my stuff together. You guys go, have fun," I said, unemotionally. My dad gave me a sideways look. "Please," I stressed.

"Suit yourself, but I guarantee you'll regret it, feel free to come join later," my dad said, walking out the door with Clay. My mom was on her way to follow them when she faltered for a minute and looked back at me.

"You gonna be okay here?" she asked.

"I'll be fine," I said. "You guys have a fun night." I turned abruptly and started grabbing clothes from my closet to busy myself until my mom left the room. I watched out the window until I saw them pass across and make their way to the hoedown. As it grew darker, the outside lights shone brighter and I could hear the gentle cords of another George Strait song.

16

Once again, I sat with Clay in the back seat, staring out the window as my parents jabbered away with Tripp, talking loudly over the radio. The same airport ride I'd taken my whole life, only this time, when we left the ranch, there was no one there to say good-bye. As a tear fell, I didn't reach up to wipe it; just let the salty drop hug between my right eye and the window glass.

*   *   *

Taking my seat on the plane and tucking my bag between my feet, I leaned over to pull out my copy of *Our Town*, alongside a tan notebook, my name printed in sharpie on the inside cover. I flipped open to the middle pages and stared at what I had thought my written response to the play would be. A carefully worded and precisely organized essay that outlined and analyzed the play through and through, the type of writing I knew would earn me an A. I pulled my pen out from the top of the notebook and drew thick lines across every sentence, page after page, until they were all gone. I flipped a few more pages in and smoothed down the middle, a clean, fresh sheet. I picked my pen back up and for the first time ever, didn't think it all through, didn't analyze every word and comma, I just wrote.

Welcome to Our Town. A town where love is simple and family comes first. A town where the littlest things, are the biggest things. But in this town, they don't think of them as little, for they recognize, that it is these so-called "little things", which take up such great room in our hearts.

Emily Webb, one of the play's central characters, comes back to her home of Grover's Corners in the form of a ghost. She watches, helplessly, as a day of her teenage life passes by without anyone taking notice. As she relives the moments as an invisible bystander, she begs herself, her parents, her brother, to look at each other, to look at the world, to take notice of all the beautiful, little, things while they can. She realizes that the things we perceive as "big" in the moment typically end up lacking importance, or even substance. Once in a lifetime may make a great memory, but it's the small, every day things we miss the most. For it's not about the grades, it's about the learning, it's not about the wedding, it's about the marriage, and it's not about the accomplishments, it's about the happiness. Sadly for Emily, this revelation comes too late, it resides in her death as deep longing, knowing that while alive, she never took notice of the things and moments that gave her true happiness and peace.

As Thornton Wilder himself said: "We can only be said to be alive in those moments when our hearts are conscious of our treasures." If this is so, then how many people who are living, are truly alive? And for the percentage who aren't, do they have any understanding of the difference? There's beauty in simplicity, you look for too much and you'll never find enough, if you let go and stop looking, you'll have more than you ever need. How much does a person miss and pass by as they are looking? Are they conscious of what they're doing? Do they think that they like and believe these things just because others tell them to? Do they live and wander without a purpose, unaware of the passions inside them? How many people expect their happiness to be found in the same place as others? And how many people spend their entire lives looking and searching, for nothing in particular?

I looked at my wrist, where the scrap metal still resided, sighing as I turned it, admiring each bit of rust that had been collected.

We overcomplicate forever, when really it is all our heart yearns for.

Days passed slowly, and as the end of each one approached, I couldn't recount what had happened, what I had done, what I had said. Everything blurred together without meaning or purpose. I went on with the routine of school but little else occupied my time, and none of it seemed to hold significance.

I sat at the foot of my bed, scribbling down answers to my last set of math problems. Placing the pen in my mouth, I gathered the worksheets and graph paper, shuffling them together to go in the sleeve of my binder.

"Rev?" my mom called from behind the door.

"Yeah?" I called out quietly. Instead of answering, she waltzed into the room and stood in front of me.

"Yes?" I asked, irritably.

"Nothing, I just haven't seen you since I got back from work," she said.

"I've been here, I wanted to get my work done," I said straightly.

"You're a senior in high school, with a month 'til graduation, how much work can you have?" she asked, picking up one of the books from my bed.

"Actually a lot," I said defensively, snatching back the book.

"Okay Rev, what's going on?" my mom said. "You've been off and moody ever since we got back from the ranch."

"I have not," I said, scowling.

"Fine," she said, "Don't talk to me," slamming the door as she walked out. I shut my eyes forcibly and put my head down on the stack of books.

"So we have to go back to all our favorite spots before Rev leaves, we have to go back to that little ice cream shop with the fountain, we have to go biking along the river, there's that upcoming class pool party, oh and we have to go prom dress shopping! Can we do that after school today?" Brenn asked jumping up and down, notebook in hand.

"I have soccer at 5:30, so I can do it if we go immediately after last period," Leslie replied. They both looked to me.

"I'll go with you guys to shop but don't count on me buying anything. I'm not gonna go to prom."

"What?" Brenn said.

"Since when?" Leslie added.

"I don't know, I've just been picturing it, and dancing and music and spinning couples and I don't know. I'm just not really into it, I guess."

"You've always loved dances," Leslie said.

"Is this because of Mitt?" Brenn asked, hand on hip.

"No, no, I swear it's not," I said honestly and yet unconvincingly. "It just doesn't really sound fun this time."

"Well it's not like we're doing the whole date thing anyway, the three of us were supposed to go together! Come on! Please!" Brenn begged.

"At least consider it," Leslie looked at me.

"Okay," I consented. "Regardless, I still wanna be there when you guys get your dresses, so I'll meet you guys in the lot after school, yeah?" I asked, starting to go back in the direction of my next class.

"See you there," Leslie said, Brenn nodding enthusiastically right beside her.

"That's the one! No doubt about it," Brenn cheered.

"Agreed," Leslie said.

"Guys stop, I'm not buying anything, I'm not even going!" I said.

"Then why'd you put it on?"

"You made me! You pulled it off the rack, shoved me in a room and took my car keys," I said, hand on hip.

"Yeah, I guess I did do that," Leslie said. Brenn laughed; I laughed too, turning to look in the mirror. It was all lace, flaring out above my knee, a dark crème color fading into blush. I ran my hands along the fabric, twirling my fingers in circles around each individual rosebud entwined in the lace. I bit my lip, remembering doing the same thing when I first put on my skirt for the hoedown at the ranch. I caught Leslie studying me through the corner of the mirror. I ran my hand through my hair and quickly got off the pedestal, marching back to the dressing room, avoiding her gaze. Hurriedly, I unzipped the dress and peeled it off, placing it back on the hanger. After pulling my jeans and T-shirt back on, I went out to the main area and sat on the couch next to Leslie. They both looked at me but I didn't wait for them to say anything,

"Brenn you should try some more on," I insisted. "Like that one," I pointed at a red dress on the rack to our left. She got up slowly and picked it off the bar.

"This one?" She held it against her body and looked down at the falling tulle.

"Yeah, it will look great on you," I said. "It's simple but it stands out, and the bright color will look great against your skin. Brenn held it out to look at thoughtfully.

"I'll try it," she said with growing excitement, then heading towards the dressing rooms. As soon as she'd left the main room, Leslie turned to me.

"You got anything else to say?" she asked.

"Nope," I said, "I was just tired of trying on dresses that I'm not gonna buy." I didn't look her in the eye.

Brenn came back out with the dress on, walking confidently towards the mirrors. It flowed gently across the curves of her body and seemed to fly out behind her as she glided past us. When she got up on the pedestal and saw herself for the first time, her smile grew until her cheeks hit the bottoms of her eyes. She twirled and started giggling gleefully.

"I love it," she said, then turning to look at herself again, "I feel pretty."

"Well you don't look pretty," Leslie said. I looked at her in shock and saw the sadness creep into Brenn's eyes. "Or I guess I should say, you don't *just* look pretty because," she paused. "You are beautiful." Brenn's eyes softened and she smiled at the ground.

"Thanks, Les," she said. I smiled as I watched her look back up and stand tall with confidence.

"You should get it," I said.

"Yeah I think I will," she looked at me thoughtfully, "But you should too."

"Brenn, come on, no, I came here for you, not me."

"And you helped me! Now reward yourself and do something for you," she smirked.

"Okay guys, I'm done with this argument. I'm not going." I got off the couch, took my keys from Leslie's bag, and left the store.

19

"It's signing day!" I woke up to my mom's high-pitched squeal, and the echoing sound of my dad's shoes against wood flooring. I sat up, rubbing my eyes, trying to make sense of the two blurs standing before me.

"We got you a little something for the big day," my mom smiled, sitting at the foot of the bed and placing a gift bag on the covers above my lap. I looked at them, confused as I pulled out pieces of blue and white tissue paper. Reaching into the bag I surfaced a bright blue sweatshirt with the Duke logo in bold across the center.

"Wow, thank you," I said, biting my lip as I traced my finger along the letters.

"We just thought that you should be in spirit for the signing," my mom said. "We're so excited the day is finally here!"

"Now try it on!" my dad said enthusiastically. I pushed my arms through and pulled it down over my head, moving my hair to fall across my back. My parents watched me with proud smiles.

"It fits," I said looking down. "Thank you again, it means a lot."

"Of course," my mom said. "Now let's see, you have the sweatshirt, you can use that special Duke pen we got you, and please make sure you get lots of pictures at the signing. We really want to see and –"

"Wait," I looked at them. "What do you mean I need to take pictures so you can see? Are you not coming?"

"Oh no sweetie, I'm sorry, didn't I tell you?" my mom asked with half-hearted concern on her face. "I just have way too much to get done at work and your father will be in a lunch meeting, so neither of us will be able to make it. I really thought I told you, are you sure I didn't?"

"Yes, I'm sure," I said coldly.

"Well I'm sorry about that, but no worries, we'll celebrate tonight," she said, putting her hand on my arm.

"Of course we will," my dad joined in. "We're both going to be home for dinner tonight and we'll make you whatever you want."

"Don't bother," I said under my breath. "Listen, thank you for the sweatshirt but if it's okay I really need to start getting my stuff together for school."

"Right, it's getting late, go ahead and get ready," my mom said, kissing my forehead. My dad followed her out as he called behind him, "We'll see you tonight." They closed my door behind them and I groaned into my pillow, not getting up until I had to leave.

20

While switching out books from my fuchsia-colored bag, I caught sight of myself in the mirror which adorned the back wall of my locker. I stared at it for a minute, examining the tired expression on my face, the pain in my eyes. Then, looking at what I was wearing, the pain appeared to deepen. I let go of my bag, letting it drop to the ground. I pulled the sweatshirt over my head, balled it together, threw it in my locker and smoothed down the black tank-top I wore underneath as an expression of ease crossed my face.

I turned to make my way into Widman's classroom and get settled in my seat, but just minutes after the bell rang, a buzz went off over the loudspeaker: "Good afternoon students," our Principal's voice was loud and friendly. "For those of you participating in today's signing ceremony, we're going to have you leave your classes early, and make your way towards the gym so that we're all set up and ready to go when the parents arrive at the end of school. See you there." The dial tone went off and Mrs. Widman gazed around the room looking for students who had to go.

"Rev, you'll be signing today won't you?" she asked.

"Uh, yeah," I said, gathering my things and walking to the front of the room. She held her finger up and turned to her desk, shuffling through a stack of crisp white papers.

"Wait, one second," she said, narrowing the pile until she found the particular stapled packet she had been searching for. "Go ahead and take this, I was going to hand them out at the end of class, it's your written response to *Our Town*." I took it from her hand and slipped it into the top pocket of my binder.

"Thank you, have a good weekend," I said on my way out.

"You too and congratulations," she said.

Walking through the doors of the gym I was placed in a long line to the side of the tables. One-by-one, students slowly began receiving information packets and seating placements, dictated by school not person. After finding my own seat, I glanced around the room, realizing how few people I knew the names of and even fewer that I actually knew. Strange to think that you can grow up alongside strangers without ever even caring enough to introduce yourself. I turned to my right and smiled at the girl sitting next to me.

"Hi!" I said, sticking out my hand. "I'm Rev."

"Mallory," she said, shaking my hand tentatively.

"Are you going to Duke too?"

"Dartmouth," she said sharply.

"Wow, congrats, that's amazing, you must be so excited," I said.

"Eh, whatever, I wanted Yale but I guess it'll do," Mallory responded, unenthusiastically.

"Dartmouth is a great school though," I insisted. "You should be proud, seriously."

"Tell my parents that," she laughed. "Anyway, it doesn't really matter, it gets me a degree and a job, and that's what it's all about, right?"

"Uh, yeah, right."

Teaching assistants and volunteer staff members began collecting the signing packets at the front of the room and asked students to prepare their materials as parents gathered outside. I hoisted my bag onto my lap and began rifling in search of a pen, when I pulled out the packet Mrs. Widman had handed me on my way out of class. The first page was a score sheet, and right at the top, in bold ink, A+. I blinked in surprise. Mrs. Widman's a hard grader and I consistently received B's on essays that I had spent days laboring over. And here, a response I'd written in less than the time of my plane flight, received a perfect score. I scanned the sheet until I saw an arrow indicating comments were written on the backside of the page. I flipped it over, and began reading.

Dear Rev,

Our community and society as a whole are often extremely driven towards work and material success, which is fine for some, but many forget to stop and think about what gives them true happiness: true, lifelong happiness, not temporary highs – they may feel exhilarating at the time but it is the small everyday moments that make up a life, not the big ones – this is a message I hope to stress and one I feel is well portrayed in my favorite play, Our Town – of all my students, your written response showed me that you had the greatest grasp on the deeper meaning of the simple text Thornton Wilder has so brilliantly written – I hope that you apply what you've learned and written to your own life, so that you may, as you wrote, live having found your true happiness and peace, wherever that may lie.

A chill went up my spine as I finished and followed it by re-reading my own words. I felt the intensity of my echoing voice, how real the play had become for me. With a burst of audacity, I stood up, clutching the papers against my chest.

"No, not right!" I turned to my right side. "Listen Mallory, I know I don't know you, even though I probably should, we all probably should, after all we've gone to the same schools our entire lives and never mind, I'm rambling but okay, I don't know you, and I don't your reasons for doing anything but that's not right, that's not what it's all about. Life isn't all money and jobs and grades, real life is joy and dreams and doing the things you love with the people you love. And if your career is going to do that for you and if Dartmouth is that stepping stone then go for it, good for you. But Duke sure as hell isn't going to do that for me, and my reason for going makes even less sense than yours, so you know what? I'm not going." I took a deep breath, slung my bag over my shoulder, and went straight out the door.

My hands gripped the steering wheel tightly and my eyes began to blur with tears as I neared the corner of my house. I stopped the car abruptly along the sidewalk and rushed inside, my feet pounding against the stairs as I ran to my room. Pulling the bin out from under my bed and reaching inside my left boot, I found the scrap metal and clasped it in my hand, holding it tenderly and wondering how something that appeared so worthless could mean the world in the right hands.

As I peered inside the bin, I saw that the picture from the ridge was still laid out on top of the photo album. I couldn't get myself to put it back in its holder. Laying there on the floor, I caught sight of the clock ticking past five. My breathing quickened as I realized how soon my parents could be getting home, I jumped up, leaving everything out on my floor, then rushing downstairs and out the door.

I got in my car and drove hurriedly for a few blocks until I reached the corner house with the grey porch swing. Bounding up the steps, I knocked loudly and attempted to wipe the tears from my eyes, unaware of how red and puffy they remained. The door swung open and Leslie stood there, her eyes immediately falling to concern. She shut the door quietly and grabbed my arm, leading me to sit beside her on the swing bench. I pressed my hand against its soft cream-colored cushion as I pulled my legs up to my chest, resting my chin on my knees.

"What happened?" she asked.

"I couldn't do it," my voice breaking as I said it.

"I could tell you didn't want to, but I need you to tell me why," she said, tilting her head to look me in the eye.

I told her everything, from beginning to end; about the ranch, about Duke, about my parents, about Cade. She didn't interrupt or ask questions, she just sat and listened, allowing me to get it all out.

"And to think we were worried that you were sad about your break up with Mitt," she said when I had finished. "I knew something was off but I had no idea how long it had been going on."

"I just can't believe I didn't do it, I couldn't do it! Am I crazy? It's the most amazing opportunity, one of the best programs in the country and I just gave it up. God my parents are going to kill me," I said, running my hands over my face. Leslie took my hand and looked at me.

"Your mind didn't stop you, your heart did, and I think we both know why," she said, I looked to the side, avoiding her gaze, still hesitant to admit the truth.

"Rev, you just saw Cade for the first time since you were fourteen, you just broke up with Mitt a few weeks ago and you'd been dating for two years. He never made your eyes light up the way they do when you talk about Cade."

"I know! We *just* broke up, and he's such a great guy. I literally have nothing negative to say about him, I should still be devastated!" I said, looking at her with pleading eyes as if she could change how I felt.

"How can you be devastated over a guy you were never in love with?" she asked me with a sympathetic smile.

"I agree that Mitt is awesome and I wish him all the best as I know you do, but you were never able to really give your heart to him and as much as you want to pretend that you're 'just not a feeling's person'," she made air quotes at the phrase I had told her a thousand times. "Think about how you feel about Cade – anyone could fall for Mitt, but you didn't, because you'd already fallen for somebody else, a long time ago," she said softly.

"You were never all in with him," she continued. "I saw it and so did he, why do you think he acted as though the breakup was "mutual"? He loves you Rev, he really does, but he knew beneath it all, you didn't feel the same way," she looked at me knowingly and my eyes found the ground shamefully, as I knew she was right.

"And on another topic," she started. "Feelings for Cade aside, you don't want to go to Duke, you never did. You've wanted the same thing since you started going to that ranch. That's the life you want so that's the life you should live and your parents will learn to live with it."

As I came back through my front door an eerie silence echoed throughout my house. I knew my parents were back yet I couldn't hear or see any evidence of their presence. I made my way up to my room where I found my mom sitting on the edge of my bed with my bin of ranch stuff in her lap. I cleared my throat as I remained in the doorway, trying to read her expression. When she realized I wasn't going to be the first to say something, her eyes narrowed.

"Is there a reason this stuff was making a mess on your floor?"

"No," I said weakly.

"Is there a reason you weren't here when we got back from work when we specifically carved out time and came home early just for you?" she asked sternly. A flash of anger took over me at the ungratefulness she was implying.

"No," I said again.

"Well then, is there a reason you didn't sign the papers to go to Duke?"

"Mom, I—--"

"You gave up the biggest opportunity of your life? What you've been working towards for years?"

"I---"

"I, don't want to hear it," she snapped back. "I've already called admissions and explained to them that you were too sick to attend the signing ceremony. I apologized on your behalf and your spot has been restored, you will officially accept with the rest of your classmates in two weeks." She moved the bin to the floor and shoved it under the bed as she stood up. "Dinner is in a half hour. I expect both myself and your father to receive an apology then." She walked out and shut the door. I stood there, hugging my arm, a mix of anger and emptiness swirling inside me as a single tear fell down my cheek.

I sat on my bed, doodling in a notebook mindlessly, a deep-weighted pain in my chest, when I heard a knock on the door. I made my way downstairs and opened it to find Leslie standing there, with Brenn right behind her. Brenn complemented her red dress with black lace heels, her short dark hair worn down with a single strand tucked behind her ear and sparkles surrounding her brown eyes. In sharp contrast, Leslie had her hair in a ponytail, a clean face, and was sporting a dark blue romper. They both looked beautiful.

"We brought you something," Leslie said. Brenn stepped out to the side, a dress bag in hand. She unzipped it to reveal the same rosebud dress I'd fallen for at the store.

"How? When did you---"

"After I talked to you, I realized why you didn't want to go to the dance," Leslie said. "I decided that wasn't a good enough reason. So," she smiled, "We're going."

"Guys I don't know," I said.

"Well we do," Leslie started, "The three of us don't have much time left together."

"We don't even have to dance if you don't want to," Brenn added.

"But your senior prom is something you need to see," Leslie said. I hesitated for a minute before looking at the dress again and then up at them. I smiled and pulled them into a hug.

"I love you guys."

"We love you too," Leslie said.

"Now go get that dress on," Brenn said, "Because it looks annoyingly good on you," she laughed. I grabbed the bag and ran upstairs with it, the two of them following at their own pace.

I shed my clothes and slipped into the dress, gazing in the mirror with a growing smile. I twirled side to side, loving the way it felt and loving that despite what I was feeling, I was going to the dance after all. For a moment, I felt like myself again, and it was the best feeling.

"Ready?" Leslie asked, peeking her head around the door.

"Yeah," I said, turning to walk out. As I went to grab my purse off my dresser, there lay the metal bracelet, in the same spot where I picked it up every night. With little hesitation and mixed emotions I slipped it over my wrist and joined my friends, linking arms with Leslie on one side, and Brenn on the other.

*   *   *

Walking into the dance, there was beautiful greenery falling from the ceiling and lanterns framing a "moonlight path" in the direction of the open floor. I gulped when I saw the bright star decorations hanging from the ceiling and felt Leslie give my hand a squeeze.

The building was crowded on all ends with my classmates, joyously dancing one of their last high school nights away. I saw Mitt from across the room and left my friends to go talk to him.

"Hey Mitt," I said, leaning back into my wedged sandal.

"Rev, you look beautiful," he said with a lonely smile.

"And you look as handsome as always," I said, then glancing at the ground. "I owe you an apology."

"What for?" he asked.

"For not being the person for you, for not being all in," I admitted out loud for the first time. "I wanted to be, I really did, but I couldn't. I couldn't let go and I wasn't honest with myself about that. All that aside, our relationship meant so much to me, getting to be with someone as great as you. You are seriously the most genuinely good person I've ever met, you deserve the absolute world, and I know that you have an amazing future ahead of you. I wish that I could be part of it but I know that I don't deserve that. You'll always have a special place in my heart." I looked him in the eye. "I'm sorry." I paused for a second before turning away to leave. He reached out and touched my arm.

"Rev," he took my hand. "I love you, I always have, and I will love you as a friend if that's what you want because I know, no matter what, I still want you to be in my life."

"Really?" I asked, my heart starting to feel full again.

"Of course," he pulled me into a hug and joy filled my body as I realized I had my friend back.

A new song came on and immediately the entire feeling of the dance changed with the slowing beat.

"You want to dance?" Mitt asked, "As friends?"

"I would," I started. "But I have some friends I came here with and I really owe it to them to have this night together." Mitt looked over my shoulder with the familiar feeling of Brenn and Leslie lingering.

"And I know your friends, so I'll leave you alone," he laughed. "But I'm glad things are okay again, I really missed you," he said.

"I missed you too." He tapped my shoulder as he brushed past me, allowing for Brenn and Leslie to run up next to me. They each grabbed an arm as they pestered me over whether I was okay.

"The most okay I've been in a long time," I smiled. "Let's dance."

*   *   *

At the end of the night Leslie was dropping me off back home when she looked at me seriously. "I really wanted tonight to be fun and light hearted but I need to know how you're doing. Are you and your mom talking yet?"

"No," I said quietly. "We've been avoiding each other, my dad's a little better but not much."

"I think you should talk to her."

"Leslie—--"

"I know it's hard and I know how you feel but I also know you talked to Mitt tonight and felt a million times better."

"Yeah well Mitt's a little softer at heart than my mom," I said.

"You're her daughter Rev; you know the silence is just as hard for her as it is for you. Talk to her. Tell her what you're feeling, how she's made you feel. If she chooses to keep being mad after that, it's her problem. But you know what? You're 18, we graduate high school in a week and tomorrow, people are signing off on what they're doing next. This part of our life is over, what do you want the next part to be?"

With Leslie's words in mind, I shut the front, door and kept moving towards my mom's office before I could stop myself. I didn't knock, just opened the door and stood in front of it. My mom peered up from a stack of papers on her desk.

"Mom," I said. "I need to talk to you."

Before I could think about what to say, everything came pouring out, with only short breaths in between.

"You asked me why I didn't sign the Duke papers. It wasn't because I was stressed out in the moment or had a change of heart, it's not because I was sick like you told admissions. I didn't sign them because I didn't want to. Because I don't want to go to Duke and I never did. What I want is to go to the ranch, to work there, to live that kind of life, that's what I've always wanted! Not to go to some fancy school and pay for a degree I don't care about. That's what I've always wanted . . . but I buried those feelings and spent the past four years trying to forget about them, ignore them. But after last month, going back to the ranch, I don't want to ignore them anymore. I want to live that same life I've always wanted. And I know you were mad when I told you that Mitt and I weren't together anymore because you think he's the perfect guy and he is, but I don't love him. I love Cade. I've loved him since we were kids. I told myself I didn't because I knew it wasn't what you wanted. Don't you think I know why we stopped going to the ranch? It started out as just a family vacation but you saw how much I loved it and how much I loved him and you didn't want me to. And I knew that, so I pretended I didn't feel that way and I hurt him in the process. I hurt someone I love, because I wanted you to love me and be proud of the life I wanted to live. You've put so much pressure on me to follow exactly in your "perfect" footsteps but I don't want to do that anymore. I love you but you put your career and your status above your family and if that's what you want to do, fine, but I'm done pretending like it's what I want. I was going to Duke for you and you couldn't leave the office for long enough to see me sign the papers. That's why I didn't sign the papers, and that's why I'm not going to sign the papers. So go ahead and call in advance telling admissions that I'm sick or hurt or in the hospital, whatever you want, cause it's not going to change anything. I'm not going."

Looking into the mirror, I pulled my hair into a low braid, holding my graduation cap over to see how it would fit. Once satisfied, I smoothed out my floral sundress and pulled on the thick blue robe.

There was a knock on the corner of my open door and through the mirror I saw my mom leaning against it as she looked at me in my cap and gown.

"After all these years," she said. "Hard to believe this day is here."

I turned but didn't make a move to say anything. We hadn't spoken in the week since I had gone into her office.

"Here," she said, walking over. "Your tassel is on the wrong side." She reached up and moved it. "It starts on the right side of your cap, and then once you've received your diploma, you move it to the left."

"Thanks," I said, looking in the mirror.

She waited a minute before saying anything more, then she just rested a hand on my shoulder and spoke to me softly.

"You're right," she said. "You're right about the pressure and about the acceptance and about where my priorities have been. And as you know, I'm not good at admitting to my own misdoings but I'm sorry and you deserve to hear that."

"I just want to know why," I swallowed. "Why I've never been good enough."

"Oh honey, it wasn't you, you've always been more than good enough." She brushed a strand of hair behind my ear. "As to why, I don't really know, all I can say is I want you to have a good life and this life gave me your father, you and Clay. To me that's pretty good. I haven't had to have too many worries and I didn't want you to either."

"Everyone has worries," I said. "They're just different kinds."

"And you have the right to choose your kind," she said. "You've shown so much greatness and I know you will continue that in whatever way you choose."

"You've never said that before," I said; she smiled sadly.

"I know, and there's a lot I could question about my parenting, but one thing I don't question is that I love you, and I am proud of you, so proud of you, whether I've shown it or not."

"So why now?"

"You made me listen. You made me look at things I didn't want to look at and you stood your ground." She looked at me thoughtfully. "You're such a strong girl, independent, capable, loving. You're right, I did choose this lifestyle and it was right for me but you're also right that what is right for me, does not mean what is right for you. I trust you to make your own life however you want it. You know better than anyone what will make you happy and what feels right in your heart. I want you to follow that."

"Really?" I asked, for the first time turning completely towards her and letting go of my stiff exterior.

"Yes really," she smiled, pulling me into a hug. When she let go, she pulled her phone out of her pocket and handed it to me.

"I think you know what you need to do," she said. I smiled when I saw the number on the phone and pressed "call." The dial tone clicked on and I heard the greeting on the other end of the phone.

"Layton, it's Rev, I have something I need to talk to you about. . ."

26

For what felt like the hundredth time, I sat in the back of a cab, winding its way through the Gallatin Gateway. As we neared the ranch, the driver turned the radio dial and once again, Randy Travis' voice was my entrance music. I bit my lip in anticipation. As we pulled onto the gravel road I told the driver he could leave me off. I thanked him and jumped out of the cab. Dragging my bag behind me, I rushed to the front office. The door slapped back against the frame as I burst towards the desk where Layton sat. She saw me and immediately got up for a hug, a huge smile on her face.

"I can't tell you how happy your call made me," she hugged me tight. "But I hope you know I expect a lot more details than the ones I got."

"Of course," I reassured her.

"Did you call the school?" she asked.

"Yes," I said excitedly. "Because of how late it is, I have to wait a semester, but after that I will be enrolled and it's only a half hour drive from here so I can easily be both a student and a wrangler."

"Sounds like everything worked out perfectly," she said with pride.

"I hope so, but there's still something I have to do," I said. "Where's Cade?"

"I don't know, he's been weird all day, he knew this was the day your program started. I saw him a couple hours ago, he said he was going out riding, said he needed to clear his head?"

"Never mind," I said, "I know where he is."

*　　　*　　　*

It didn't take long for me to reach the Ridge. On the way up, I refused to waste a second, keeping Grayling at a fast pace the whole time. Cade sat with his back to me, staring out at the spot where the sky meets the valley. I tied Grayling next to Gallatin, still about thirty yards away. I walked up quietly, then breaking the silence. I saw his back stiffen at my voice.

"I still know my way here, and I'm done trying to forget it," I said. He turned and stood, looking at me standing there with a shock-ridden expression. His shirt was rumpled and his workout shorts baggy, the same outfit he regularly slept in. My eyes were sharp while his still looked mildly bloodshot. We stared at each other for a few minutes, still a good ten feet apart.

"What are you doing here?" he said finally.

"Trying to take back the life I really want," I said. I was the first to step forward, "Everything you said was right. I love it here, I love this life, and I love you. I'm sorry it's taken me so many years to come to terms with that." He looked at me and moved forward.

"You're not going?" he asked.

"I'm not going anywhere," I said. I saw him look down and he picked up my wrist where the scrap metal remained.

"It's forever," I shrugged, my eyes beginning to water. He looked down at me and smiled, pulling me into his embrace.

He kissed the top of my head and whispered "I love you too."

Together we walked forward towards the edge where we sat, hand-in-hand, in the grasses.

"Quartz had her baby," he said. "It's a girl."

"What'd you name her?" I asked.

"We haven't yet, got any ideas?"

"I don't know, I---" my voice trailed off as I gazed out at the beauty of the landscape, the openness of the sky, then I smiled. "Ridge," I said; Cade looked at me. "You should name her Ridge. That way she can't ever forget."

Cade nodded thoughtfully, looking into my eyes, then smiling to himself.

"Ridge it is."

Made in the USA
San Bernardino, CA
20 December 2019